C000163184

Neither Tutsi, Nor Hutu

A Rwandan Memoir

*My Search for Healing, Meaning, and Identity
after Witnessing Genocide and Surviving Civil War*

By Prosper Ishimwe

MODERN MEMOIRS, INC.
Amherst, Massachusetts

Neither Tutsi, Nor Hutu: A Rwandan Memoir; My Search for Healing, Meaning, and Identity after Witnessing Genocide and Surviving Civil War
© 2020 Prosper Ishimwe

All rights reserved. No part of this book may be reproduced, stored in a retrieval system, or transmitted in any form or by any means—electronic, mechanical, photocopying, recording, or otherwise—without prior written consent of the copyright owner.

The thoughts, opinions, and events expressed in this book are those of the author and are based upon the author's recollections and research related to the subject matter herein. The author takes full and sole responsibility for its contents and regrets any content that might be construed as injurious to anyone mentioned or implied.

This book has been published privately in the United States.
Cover design by Vinsula Hastings, with the author.

Front cover image:
The author as a baby, held by his cousin Bonaventure, near the house where he was born, Karembo, Rwanda (around 1987). This is the author's only picture that survived the looting and destruction of property during and after the genocide and war.

Back cover images:
Map of Rwanda, retrieved from www.africaguide.com, accessed 03/19/20.
"Selective Focus of Banana Leaves" photo by Elina Sazonova from Pexels.
Author photo: Prosper Ishimwe, in Washington, D.C. (around 2016).

ISBN: 978-1-09831-529-0
To contact the author, please email:
NeitherTutsiNorHutu@gmail.com

For more copies of this book, please visit:
Store.Bookbaby.com OR
Store.Bookbaby.com/book/neither-tutsi-nor-hutu

MODERN MEMOIRS, INC.
34 Main Street #6
Amherst, MA 01002
www.modernmemoirs.com
413-253-2353

This book is dedicated to all victims of genocides and wars,
including my mom, my little sister Petite, my cousins Kennedy and
Mapua, my grandfather Yakobo, and also to those
who choose fair-mindedness and forbearance
despite surviving the unimaginable.

CONTENTS

PREFACE

If you've met a Rwandan, you've likely told them, "Oh! I watched the movie *Hotel Rwanda*!" And perhaps you followed up with something like, "It's so tragic how horrible human beings can be to other human beings. But I am glad you survived and are safe."

After getting to know them a little more, maybe you asked, "So, are you Hutu or Tutsi?" This question very likely made them uncomfortable, or maybe it startled them, and made the conversation a bit awkward.

Many Rwandans, especially younger ones, would likely answer such a question by saying, "I am just Rwandan." Perhaps such a response was confusing to you, since you were very certain that Rwandans were divided into Hutus and Tutsis— and maybe you'd even heard of the Twa people. If you are familiar with Africa, perhaps you thought that tribal identity was something Africans were comfortable talking about.

The truth is that tribal or "ethnic" labels in Rwanda were discouraged by the new government in the aftermath of the civil war, in an attempt to forge a national identity, and whether this attempt has been successful is still up for debate. Furthermore, "ethnic" identification (notice that I put this word in quotation marks to indicate its speciousness) in Rwanda is much more complicated than it is anywhere else in Africa. By writing this book, I hoped to explore why this is so, as a means of better understanding how and why the 1994 genocide occurred in my country, when I was just eight years old. By doing so, I hope to illuminate the complexity of identity in Rwanda for you, too.

Writing this book has been the most rewarding experience of my three decades of life. It is the culmination of a lifelong struggle to break free from the confines of a culture that seemed to expect everyone to do the same things, the same way. My rebelliousness started well before my teenage years. I was frustrated that not enough people were trying to address all the contradictions and illogical practices I saw around me. Many things simply did not make sense to me, so I was in constant conflict with my culture, my polity, and my Catholic religion.

I must say that my father, although he has a different personality than I, understood me better than many people. He let me become my true, unique self despite our stiflingly conformist culture, which was at odds with my renegade personality. He would always tell me, "Prosper, tu es *trop liberal!*", meaning I was too liberal. I knew he understood me, and although he's never told me so, I knew he was (and still is) worried for my safety and happiness.

Choosing to leave my motherland in 2014 to live in the United States was a way for me to avoid not just conformist suffocation in Rwanda, but my own endangerment and that of my family. Though the genocide took place two decades earlier, in 1994, its political reverberations are felt to this day. Leaving Rwanda allowed me to live in a place where I could be myself and heal and reckon with my past without clashing with my culture, my religion, and especially my political leaders. In America, I hoped to find people who understood me, and I thought the "land of the free and the home of the brave" would be a perfect ecological niche for me. (I will share about my experiences in America in my second book, forthcoming.)

When I started writing, I was unaware of the hardships of book publishing. Most people I approached took my story as a product, and so did publishing companies. Some of my American friends would even say things like, "You have such a great story!" because it seemed as if it had the makings of a Hollywood movie that would make me rich and popular. I was not offended, but these comments were painful. I have also encouraged a few people to write their own stories and they would say things like, "My story is not as interesting." One of them even wished she had a story like mine. Can you imagine?

I quickly understood that these friends' worldviews were different than mine, since they'd grown up in a Hollywood-dominated culture. To them, the stories I shared were things that happened on the screen, not to real people they knew, so upon meeting me and hearing about my life, they could only place me in the context of a "badass" celebrity. To be fair, the response from most people was that of genuine empathy even when they did not know the right way to sympathize (and it was not that different from stoic Rwandans who resisted looking at the past).

Ultimately, I decided to self-publish. I had been trying to grow out of my perfectionism, and I realized this would be a great way to do so. I was able to turn over my writing to an editor and book designer while maintaining control over how I wanted to share my story. I also wanted to use my own story to embark on a journey aimed at encouraging people to share their stories in whatever form they like. Someone's story may involve tragedy of the same proportion as mine, or not; that story may undergo work with an editor, or not; a commercial publishing house may give a writer a contract, or not. No matter what, I know that everyone has a story that is worth telling.

Therefore, as you start this tour of my past with me—a journey of growing up in a divided society, living through tragedy, and making peace with the past—I hope you will appreciate my vulnerability and my offering of my piece of humanity's puzzle, with all its dents. Then, I *especially* hope you will be inspired to share your story with the world without self-judgment. Offer yourself to the world the way you are, with your brokenness and fortitude, with your unique past, and your peculiar DNA that makes you different from *anyone else* in the world. This uniqueness constitutes, I believe, your true contribution and gift to the richness of the world.

It is by telling our stories that we will find the answers to life's biggest questions, and that we will come to the realization of our oneness.

As the saying attributed to Pablo Picasso goes, "The meaning of life is finding your gift. The purpose of life is to give it away." My gift to you is this account of my life and my three-decade journey. I hope you receive it with an open heart and will feel inspired to tell your own story because I believe it is by sharing stories that we create the empathy necessary to build peace and unity.

Finally, to my fellow Rwandans who, like me, were children during the genocide and war, and especially to those born after 1994:

I hope you will give yourselves permission to tell your stories in their wholeness. Most importantly, I pray that you will regard our country's tragic history with the full strength of your critical minds so that we may boldly take charge of our motherland's destiny. I believe this destiny will be shaped by our collective ability, or inability, to empathize with all Rwandans. Such empathy will be at the heart of true reconciliation, enabling us to forge genuine bonds strong enough to withstand divisive political manipulation and ethno-nationalist propaganda.

Gratefully,
Prosper Ishimwe
Providence, Rhode Island
2020

INTRODUCTION: A BRIEF HISTORY OF "INTER-ETHNIC" CONFLICT IN RWANDA

Conflict is the beginning of consciousness.
—M. Esther Harding

The history of Rwanda, like that of many parts of the world, has been marred by "inter-ethnic" power struggles. Grievances create an endless cycle of victims turning into victimizers. In my opinion, the main obstacle to Rwandan unity and reconciliation before and after the 1994 genocide, is a lack of humility and empathy on behalf of radicals. This failing has engendered a hierarchy of oppression in which whoever is in power ranks the grievances of those belonging to their ethnic group as most important, sometimes ignoring the suffering of those on the other side. It follows that the group that is not in power feels dominated and oppressed.

The Tutsis and Hutus are the two major Rwandan social groups. Whether they are understood or referred to as socioeconomic classes, tribes, or distinct "ethnic groups," they managed to form one national identity, dating back to the fourteenth century CE. It is unclear whether small kingdoms that were annexed and subdued bore any grudges against the central government and attempted to secede during the early nation-building struggle. What *is* clear is that the Kingdom of Rwanda was relatively unified, and power was centralized, with the Tutsis and Hutus living together in apparent harmony until the arrival of European colonizers in the mid-1800s.

In the pre-colonial era, most Tutsis belonged to the Rwandan aristocracy and held more economic and political power. They occupied most leadership positions, including chiefdoms. Some accounts, however, allege that the King ceased to be Tutsi and was instead considered Rwandan as soon as he was enthroned. There's also evidence of social mobility that allowed some Hutus to acquire Tutsi status when they gained wealth and power, mostly through military prowess—a point that calls into question historical and contemporary claims of separate and stable ethnic groupings.

According to most historical writings, the Germans and the later-arriving Belgians who colonized Rwanda respected the established social hierarchy, leaving Tutsis as the leadership class and Hutus as servants. However, Belgian colonization took the step of issuing identity cards that assigned ethnicity, thus hardening identities and halting social mobility. There's consensus that the colonizers favored the Tutsi minority and used them to rule over the masses of Hutus. It's fair to surmise that the Tutsis did not consider the Hutus their equals, and one could even argue that the majority saw them as servants who were unfit and ill-equipped to lead. But this doesn't mean the Tutsis were happy with colonization, nor with their collaboration with the Germans and Belgians.

In 1961, when the Rwandan monarchy was abolished, thus eradicating an historical site of Tutsi power, many Hutus did not have consciousness of their oppression. Only a small segment of the Hutu elite who had managed to acquire formal education in Catholic schools fomented the controversial 1959 Hutu revolution, helped by Belgian colonial leaders. Indeed, it would have been impossible without the backing of Belgian Colonel Guy Logiest, who was brought in by the colonial governor after the king started to make claims for independence, as many African leaders were doing at that time. Belgian colonialists turned against the king and the Tutsis they had collaborated with for decades, and worked with the Hutu elite to bring down the monarchy. The elite of the two groups started seeing themselves as two entities competing for political supremacy in the emerging post-colonial era. "Ethnic" identity was now politicized, hardened, and polarized.

At independence in 1962, the Hutu elite took power, and instead of healing divides and sharing power, they saw it as their turn to dominate the Tutsis, thereby legitimizing their persecution. The government spearheaded a campaign to dehumanize Tutsis and portray them as an alien race that did not belong to Rwanda and that had kept the majority Hutu in servitude for centuries. Such propaganda forced several thousand Tutsis into exile after their relatives were killed and their houses burned down, and it instigated ongoing persecution of those Tutsis who did not flee the country.

Today, the Rwanda Patriotic Front (or the RPF, the current Tutsi-dominated ruling party) does not recognize the Hutu revolution because, they argue, it was masterminded and orchestrated by the Belgian colonial authorities, and mostly because of the violence and oppression Tutsis endured under the first Hutu-dominated republic, initiated after independence in 1962. Tutsis who fled to neighboring countries did not initially seek peaceful return to their country. Instead, they carried out what are called the first Inyenzi attacks on Hutu targets and the Hutu-led government, between 1962 and 1967. One attack reached a few miles from the capitol city of Kigali, polarizing the conflict and leading to retaliatory attacks on innocent Tutsis who remained in the country.

Some hold that the second Hutu republic, in the early 1970s, eased the suffering of Tutsis, but persecution and discrimination nevertheless continued, translating into policies that curtailed the rights of Tutsis in education and leadership. When Tutsi refugees asked to return to their country in the 1980s, President Juvénal Habyarimana dismissed their request, saying, "The country is full like a glass of water. If you pour more water you risk spilling even the water that was there in the first place." This rejection would be the worst blunder of his presidency. For the second time, the country missed the opportunity to heal "ethnic" divides by refusing thousands of Rwandans their innate right to return to their homeland.

Many young Tutsis in Rwanda at the time felt disempowered and marginalized and fled the country to join the Rwanda Patriotic Front (RPF), which was then a rebel movement comprised mostly of Tutsi refugees who had fled the violence in 1959 and in the years that followed. Realizing that the Hutu-dominated government under President Habyarimana would not allow them to return to their country peacefully, the RPF decided to return by force.

In 1986, in Uganda, the RPF had helped President Yoweri Museveni ascend to power, which gave them exceptional military experience. In 1990 they launched their first attack on Rwanda from the northern border with Uganda. RPF founder Fred Gisa Rwigema was killed in the fighting. After this, the Rwanda Patriotic Army (RPA) leader, Paul Kagame (who was attending a military course in the United States at the time), returned to Uganda to assume leadership of the struggle. The RPA retreated into Volcanoes National Park, in northwestern Rwanda, and launched guerrilla attacks that led to the displacement of the Hutu-majority population from the

Northern Province.

Under pressure from the international community, President Habyarimana opened the political space in 1990, leading to the formation of opposition parties. When he realized that he was not going to win the war against the RPA, President Habyarimana acquiesced to power-sharing negotiations in Arusha, Tanzania, which were initiated in June 1992. This political concession led to the birth of the notorious Hutu Power radical wings of opposition parties, whose members did not want to share power with the Rwanda Patriotic Front. These Hutu extremists embarked on a campaign to demonize all Tutsis and any moderate Hutu who opposed their agenda.

Habyarimana's political party, the National Republican Movement for Democracy and Development, also created so-called "self-defense" youth groups known as the Interahamwe militia. Today, we know that these young Hutu men were not being trained to defend their villages against the advance of the Tutsi-led Rwanda Patriotic Army, but to kill innocent Tutsis whom they considered as sympathizers and even collaborators of the RPF Tutsis.

Tutsi families with young men who had joined the rebellion were targeted by Hutu radicals. The opposition parties to President Habyarimana was weakened and divided by Hutu Power dissidents. The Hutu purists, emboldened by the fact that Hutus were the majority (84% of the population), found no need to share power with the minority Tutsi (14% of the population). President Habyarimana went ahead and signed the Arusha Peace Agreement in August 1993 with the RPF, but his inner circle (including his wife, First Lady Agathe Habyarimana, who had political power in her own right) vehemently opposed it. The RPF sent a 600-man battalion to Kigali to oversee the implementation of the power-sharing process, and the United Nations sent the UN Assistance Mission for Rwanda with a mandate to keep peace, provide humanitarian assistance, and support the ongoing peace process.

Despite these steps, the power-sharing process was delayed, and it became obvious that Hutu extremists had rejected the Arusha Peace Agreement and were planning the extermination of Tutsis, whom they called "accomplices," and moderate Hutus, whom they called "traitors." Security deteriorated and the conflict became even more polarized.

On April 6, 1994 the presidential plane was shot down as it returned from Tanzania, killing everyone on board, including President Habyarimana and President Cyprien Ntaryamira of Burundi, who also happened to be on the plane. On April 7, the Radio Television Libres des Milles Collines (RTLM), the voice of the Hutu Power propaganda machine, attributed the responsibility to the RPF and a contingent of UN soldiers, inciting the extermination of Tutsi. For the 100 days that followed, Hutu radicals, assisted by the presidential guards and the gendarmerie, carried out genocidal warfare, killing hundreds of thousands of innocent Tutsi civilians and moderate Hutus. Ordinary Hutus across the country also responded to the devilish call and murdered their neighbors, including family members in some instances.

At the same time, the Rwanda Patriotic Army (RPA) was advancing into the country, conquering territory and saving the lives of Tutsis who survived the massacres, and in some cases, indiscriminately killing civilian Hutus, including children and the elderly. Whether these killings were ordered from the top leadership of the RPA or not, we may never know; but we know that the killings were systematically organized and carried out, and in many instances the bodies of the dead were incinerated. In the former Kibungo Province, for example, entire families were rounded up in open spaces and murdered in cold blood. Some were told that they were going to attend meetings and they were indiscriminately gathered and killed.

The tragedy did not conclude with the end of the 100-day massacre. In summer 1994, the defeated Hutu-led government and Interahamwe militia who carried out the genocide against the Tutsi fled to the Democratic Republic of Congo, taking with them about 1.4 million refugees, mostly Hutus afraid of RPF retaliation. This was the start of one of the worst refugee crises of the century, with thousands of people dying of waterborne diseases. Then, in an effort to counter attacks by the defeated army that was organizing and recruiting in refugee camps to attack the country from the Democratic Republic of Congo (and then Zaïre), the new Tutsi-led Rwandan government invaded Congo. They destroyed refugee camps, killed thousands of refugees, and forced a majority of the displaced people to return to Rwanda, setting in motion what some historians call Africa's World War. At the time of the writing of this book, the Democratic Republic of Congo has not fully recovered from the intervention.

After the genocide and civil war, the victors, whether by genuine determination to unite the country and/or political pragmatism, discouraged "ethnic" identification. They were a minority political group and knew they could not hold power by playing identity politics. It was a happy coincidence in which the interests of the political elite and those of the country aligned.

Younger Rwandans, especially those born after 1994, started identifying themselves as Rwandan—at least in public.

And yet, in a country that had just suffered a genocide fueled by ethnic hatred, this was not an easy transition. The government could control what people said and did publicly, but not in private.

Those with de facto power were mostly Tutsis from the RPF who stopped the genocide, along with some Tutsis who had survived the genocide and felt the responsibility of keeping the victims' memory alive. How could they talk about the genocide without naming the victims and the perpetrators? Even younger Rwandans could infer from conversations about the genocide whether a family was from the victims' or perpetrators' group. Of course, there are nuances and grey areas, but as much as one may try to detach from lazy, dichotomous thinking, the human, reptilian brain jumps back to binary thinking, especially when we have to make decisions that involve our safety, like whom to marry or trust with our lives and wellbeing.

Coming of age in Rwanda after the genocide and civil war forced me to grapple with these questions around identity and belonging, as a means of spiritual and emotional survival.

NEITHER TUTSI, NOR HUTU:
A RWANDAN MEMOIR

PART I

MY STORY

Deciding to Tell My Story

*If there's a book that you want to read, but it hasn't been
written yet, then you must write it.*

—Toni Morrison

Brett was one of the first people I befriended after arriving
in Lewiston, Maine in 2014. He had met his wife, Marie, at Bates
College, where Marie taught French. Brett was Baha'i, and he
had introduced Marie to the Faith before they got married and
settled in Lewiston to serve inner-city youth. I called myself spiritual, but not religious, and I never imagined there was an organized religion founded on the same principles I had long known
to be true; but as Brett and Marie told me about their Baha'i
Faith, which inspired them to dedicate their lives to building
the unity of humankind, I found I believed in everything they
shared with me. Their dedication to serve the community was

awe-inspiring. I had never met anyone who shared my basic, core beliefs, and I was astounded at my good fortune in finding these kindred spirits so far from my Rwandan homeland.

My friendship with Brett led to connections with other people, and eventually to my decision to share my story of surviving the Rwandan civil war. He invited me to join what he called the Friday Youth Gathering with other friends, named Jake and Matt, at his and Marie's one-bedroom apartment on Wood Street. Brett and Matt went to Bates College, just yards away from the apartment. All of us were meaningful conversation enthusiasts, and to my mind, the Friday Youth Gathering (also called the Friday Gathering and the Friday Group) resembled Enlightenment salons where authors, thinkers, and philosophers convened for intellectual and spiritual discourse. I was new in town, yet I strangely felt at home with this Friday Group, especially with Brett and Jake. It was as if I was always meant to meet them.

Jake quickly got to know me and why I was seeking asylum in the United States. When I told him I had run away from my country because it was unsafe for me to share my story there, his face lit up. He told me he had a podcast meant to give people a platform to share their stories. It was like we were experiencing some sort of divine intervention that gave meaning to the crossing of our paths.

I knew I had to tell my story, and I was thinking of writing a book, this book, but was terrified and uncertain about whether I was ready to break my twenty-year-long silence about the crimes I had survived. I had never felt safe enough to tell my survival story, lest I get myself in trouble by upsetting the current rulers of my native land. But my love for my departed mother was so undeniably intense that I decided I could risk anything to exhume her story. I felt a quasi-destined purpose in doing so, as I determined to shed some light on the gray areas of the genocide narrative, and to hopefully contribute to the ongoing dialogue on reconciliation. My decision felt noble and bold, but I was still petrified by the risk of potential banishment from my country (a place I treasured profoundly) and of being ostracized by my people (whom I cherished so dearly).

On Christmas Eve of 2014, Jake formally asked to interview me for his podcast. It was three months after I arrived in Maine and we set the date for the interview. I did not know what questions he would ask; all I knew was that I was going to tell the truth no matter what the consequences might be. Between setting the date and the actual recording of the interview, my head was spinning with all kinds of thoughts and questions:

Will my family, all of them still in Rwanda, be hurt because of me?

Will they be tortured and forced to disown me?

Is this worth it?

What have I gotten myself into?

But deep inside, I knew that if people feared telling the truth because those with de facto power might hurt us or our loved ones, the truth would never come out. And if the truth never came out, true healing would never happen.

I told myself that if I spoke my truth, I could live with the consequences of my choice. I had never told my father or any member of my family that I was seeking asylum, nor that I was going to write a memoir about my survival story. It was my mission alone, and alone I would carry it out. I had come to the realization that my purpose on Earth was not to be safe, but to live truthfully and authentically. Telling my survival story was an integral part of realizing that purpose. It was worth dying for.

It was the reason I had survived. It was my piece of the puzzle, my contribution to the world: to share myself wholly and whole-heartedly with the world, both my resilient and vulnerable self.

The day came. The interview was on Skype. I took my earplugs, went to the computer room at Tree Street Youth Center, where I volunteered, and waited for Jake to call.

The interview with Jake opened a Pandora's box of emotions and memories. I knew I had to start writing my whole story. The next day, I woke up before 5:00 a.m., went to Tree Street Youth Center, sat at the computer, and started writing.

My Story Begins

I was born eight years before the 1994 genocide, in a south-eastern village in Karembo, on the slope of one of the thousand rolling green hills of Rwanda. Most memories of my childhood are happy ones.

My earliest one was when I was about four years old—if I remember correctly. My cousin Alivera was getting married. My sister, Lily, was her fille d'honneur, or flower girl. I had to stay home with the house-helper, Nirere, for some reason. Lily and I were inseparable, so when she left for the wedding, I cried. My father was home, and he took me on a motorcycle ride and bought me some cookies (or biscuits, as we called them) which was enough to calm me down. This is still one of the fondest memories I have of the good connection I've always had with my father.

I have many other fond memories of time with my father and our family. Evening family time was my favorite time of the day, except that before nightfall we had to take a cold bath, which my cousin Kennedy and I dodged whenever possible. Water was so cold in the evening, especially on the cold days of the rainy season. We would go to the shower room (or douche, as we call it), wash our heads, torsos, and legs, and get out wrapped in towels and looking as if we had taken a whole-body wash. Of course, my mother would later inspect us and make sure we had a proper shower. She was a true African matriarch and did not tolerate childish shenanigans.

While food was being prepared by Nirere, we liked to hang out in our parents' bedroom doing homework and chitchatting. When homework was done, my father would pull out his guitar and play funny songs, teasing us about our behaviors. The one that stuck with me had lyrics that consisted of telling Lily not to cry, and wishing she would not get sick again, and then a funny part of the song teased me for dancing while seated. As the music, homework, and conversations slowed down, my sisters and I would pretend to fall asleep on our parents' bed so Nirere would carry us to our beds. Then, as soon as we were laid onto our beds, we all burst into laughter, which Nirere did not like. These were precious moments when all of us were still together, enjoying each other's company.

Although I loved being with my family, I had an independent streak. I started school at the age of six even though the required age to start Primary One was seven. The other six-year-old students and I were called Ibinyoni, or Little Birds. This name was given to kids who went to school before the required age because they showed interest. There were not many preschool programs in the country, or at least not in my town. I pressured my parents every day to let me start school, and when I turned six they finally agreed, on the condition that I would behave and do well. I knew that if any Ibinyoni did not do well, they would repeat the year.

I also believe they took me to school to protect me from a potentially negative influence from my friends. Some of them were older and did not go to school because they had to help their parents on the farm and look after cows. My friends Isaiah and Kizito (or Gikeri and Kazete, as they were nicknamed), for example, had to take their father's cows grazing every day. I liked to go cattle grazing with Isaiah and Kizito. It was an exciting adventure.

I tried to find time to go with them outside of school hours, which was made easier since a shortage of classroom space and teachers meant that students from Primary One to Primary Four studied in shifts: the morning shift started from seven to twelve and the afternoon shift from two to five. But my mother required that my sisters and I take a nap every afternoon after lunch to prevent us from sleeping before dinner was ready at night. I did not like the afternoon nap at all. I was very playful, and I did not approve of how the siesta reduced my playtime. But my mother was very strict, so I could not disobey her openly. I had to learn a few tricks to ditch this non-negotiable nap.

First, I would eat lunch—during which I always had to be reminded to sit down and finish. Then I would tell Nirere that I was going to take the afternoon nap. Sometimes she would come check whether I was asleep, and I would pretend I was. She would return to the backyard to do her afternoon chores, which included a lot of cooking, cleaning, and harvesting, to mention a few tasks. When I was sure Nirere was convinced I was sleeping, I would get up and sneak out through the front door and run to Isaiah and Kizito's house. They lived down the hill from our house.

I envied Isaiah and Kizito for being able to explore nature

while grazing cows, a chore I was not allowed to do. Emmanuel, our second helper, looked after our cows, and he was Nirere's secret lover. I once walked in on them having sex, Emmanuel on the top of Nirere. They were both covered by a blanket, but as a five-year old, I still thought this was the most bizarre thing I had ever seen. My parents did not want me to hang out with them lest they teach me undesirable behaviors. Cow boys were said to use bad words and to swear. And indeed, one swear word I learned from Isaiah and Kizito was Ndagaswi, the short form for Ndagasweramama, which is the equivalent of motherfucker in English. When my mother heard me say this word, she made sure I regretted it. I had no clue what the word meant, but she beat me so hard that I understood the inappropriateness of my newly acquired vocabulary. Since that time, I have never sworn again.

When I went cattle grazing with Isaiah and Kizito, they would go to people's fields to dig sweet potatoes and roast them in an underground oven, a technique called urwubike, which is similar to Hawaiian Imu. This underground roasting was one of my favorite parts of going cattle grazing with my friends. Other escapades consisted of ripening bananas underground, and trapping and roasting partridges.

My mother did not know any of this. I knew exactly the time my parents came home from work. My father had a Suzuki motorcycle that he and my mother rode every day to work. I had mastered its peculiar sound and I would run back home as soon as I heard it, from as far as three miles away. I would sneak in the house through the front door and go to bed and pretend I was sleeping, with all the dust still on my feet. When they got home I would wait and go greet them as if I had just awoken. But of course, my adventures often left me exhausted, and I would fall asleep before dinner was ready, which told my mother that I had not taken my afternoon nap after all.

When I was not at school or hanging out with Kizito and Isaiah, I played in my paternal grandmother's front yard. My father had built her a house across from ours so he could take care of her, since she was widowed when she was still young. Everyone in the village and beyond knew Grandma for her generosity, but mostly for her profession. She was an herbalist and midwife, and she did not charge a dime for her services. A Catholic priest who had done research on traditional Rwandan medicine had taught her all of his knowledge about medicinal plants before he passed.

Her daily routine consisted of walking the forest and bush in search of medicinal plants, drying them, and preparing potions to give her patients. She had even earned the respect of modern doctors since she was licensed to treat people, and to deliver babies if laboring women could not make it to the only health center in the entire commune. When she wasn't tending her patients, who mostly showed up without appointments, she was weaving mats and baskets to give away as gifts, or to barter for sugar, salt, and bread. As she wove her mats and baskets, or made crowns from bamboo trees, she usually sang to make fun of her old age and her inability to work in the field:

> Yewe Mudahinga Nyangore, se ko utize Nyangore?
> (Now that you are too old to farm, and haven't
> attended school, Nyangore,)
> Uzatungwa n'iki Nyangore?
> (How will you support yourself, Nyangore?)
> Nzarya dukeye, noze akarenge Nyangore.
> (I will eat very little, and clean up.)

Or to marvel at how fast science and technology were advancing, and how pleased she was to witness these changes:

> Uwapfuye yarihuse, atabonye tingatinge
>> (Those who passed went too soon, before they
>> saw a tractor)
> bayitengeneza umuhanda
>> (leveling rough roads.)

Or she sang a lullaby she liked to use to soothe crying kids:

> Uhore nguhendahendeee maweeee
>> (Dear little one, please don't cry,)
> Maze nguhoze nguhetseee maweee,
>> (I will sing you lullabies as I carry you on my
>> back,)
> Nzakujyana iwanyogosengeee maweee,
>> (I will take you to see your aunt,)
> Nibakubona bazatambaaa maweee,
>> (When they see you, they will dance for you,)
> Batambane inkongorooo maweee,
>> (They will dance with gourds,)
> Zuzuye amata zoseee maweee,
>> (Gourds full of milk.)

My father told us that she paid for his secondary school tuition by making and selling bamboo crowns. It was after he graduated and got a job as a primary school teacher that he built her house next to ours. As kids, we spent our days moving between Grandma's house and our house, and she was half-deaf so when talking to her, one had to bend closer to her ear and speak loudly. Every time my father bought meat, he made sure he gave some to my grandmother, and she always had candy, bread or leftover food that she gave us, especially to thank us for helping with chores or running errands.

As for my grandfather, I never knew him. He died when my father was young himself and he has very little memory of him. His name was Kamonyo which translates to "little ant." It was considered disrespectful to mention your father-in-law by his name, and so my mom and my uncles' wives never said the word "ant." They always made up names for ants, and every one of them had her own way to refer to him.

My uncles' wives sometimes said that I resembled my grandfather and had his hair and forehead. One of them even told me she once thought she saw him when she saw me walking towards her from afar. Sadly, my grieving grandmother ripped to pieces the last picture of him, so I never got to see what he looked like. All I know is that he was strong, tall, judicious, and respected.

I did hear a few stories about my grandfather. My favorite was that he used to come home at night accompanied by a cheetah, and he would knock on the door and say, "I am with a guest," and my grandmother would throw a goat or a hen outside for the cheetah. I never asked whether the story was true, but there were other stories of people being accompanied by cheetahs. The conventional wisdom was that if you did not panic, look back, run, or change your pace, they would accompany you and leave whenever they wanted. Friend to cheetahs or not, I would have loved to know my grandfather.

My father was not the only son to look out for his widowed mother. My uncle Thomas, who was the youngest in my father's family, stayed with my grandmother before he was married. He was my godfather, and he had a cassette stereo that played very loud music. At as young as four years old, I learned to dance while listening to that loud music. One of the popular dances was to the Congolese music called Kwasakwasa. We danced to it by repeatedly making up-and-down zigzag movements.

Sunday was a special day in our extended family. We dressed up and went to mass. My mother made a special meal, which usually included beef cooked with garlic and many other culinary herbs including thyme. On Sunday, we also went to visit our cousins or friends, which I enjoyed since I got to show off my athletic and acrobatic skills learned from my cousin Kennedy from Kigali, and from the acrobats at the Gatenga Youth Center.

But by far, the most memorable time of the year was Christmas. My mother made the best mandazi (donuts) and prepared the most delicious beef and plantain dishes. Older family friends bought us lots of candy. My father built the nativity set with a manger made of cyprus leaves and small banana trees. Sometimes he used figurines, but most of the time he drew his own scene of Mary, Joseph, baby Jesus, shepherds, sheep, the three wise kings bearing gifts, and the star they followed to Jesus' birthplace. I built my own little nativity set with a manger, which I set in my room. My siblings and I all got new Christmas clothes, which I always awaited to wear for the first time with tremendous anticipation. On Christmas Eve, I had an indescribable feeling of excitement and was too excited to sleep as I looked forward to waking up. Even the sun seemed to shine in a unique way as if it was also happy to celebrate Christmas.

Childhood Home

When I sleep, and dream of home
I see the house where I grew up
The avocado and mango trees,
The banana plantations and the fields of beans,
The stables, and the animals.

My parents' bedroom where my father
Played the guitar before dinner,
The corner where he built the Christmas nativity manger,
The kitchen where my mother prepared the Christmas delicacies,
The front yard where we played soccer.

I see the path I took to school through the eucalyptus parish
    forest,
I hear the birds chirping and cheering as we barefoot walked to
    school,
I feel the warm earth beneath my feet on summer afternoons,
I miss the rainy days, and the sliding in the mud.

I hear my best friend, and cousin Kennedy sing
"Nothing's Gonna Change My Love for You" by Glenn Medeiros,
I hear the cows mooing, and chickens clucking.
The morning rooster crow, the goat bleat,
My father milking the cows on foggy mornings.

Then I wake up,
Only to realize that my home is no more.
I am thousands of miles away,
And the house which holds manifold memorable moments
Exists no more.
All I have are the ineffaceable memories I cherish
So dearly.

Things Fall Apart

We must learn to live together as brothers
or perish together as fools.

—Martin Luther King, Jr.

I spent part of my 1993 Christmas break at my uncle Mugenzi's house in Kigali. My uncle and his wife, Xaverine, were members of Parti Libéral (PL), one of the opposition parties that supported multiparty efforts and the repatriation of the Rwandan Tutsi refugees. The party's uniform was green, printed with yellow stars. While in Kigali, I was given a PL cap and shirt. When I returned home to my village with my cousin Kennedy, he and I took pride in wearing the uniform in a place where almost everyone was a member of the president's opposing party (MRND). It was a transitional period to party pluralism, and everyone was involved in one way or another in one of the parties, rallying every week to garner all the support they could get.

We had a small red TV set that displayed blurry black-and-white images, which my father purchased mainly to watch the World Cup, and of course to follow the hot news of the country's contentious transition to a multiparty system. As kids, we heard lots of songs from party rallies. Some of the figures who kept coming back in the news were Tito Rutaremara, the current ombudsman of Rwanda, and Agatha Uwiringiyimana, the then prime minister, who would be one of the first politicians assassinated after the crash of the presidential plane in April 1994.

Newspapers printed dehumanizing caricatures of political figures. One that stuck with me portrayed Kagame, the then leader of the RPA, the Tutsi-dominated rebel group that fought for the right of Rwandan refugees to return to Rwanda. In this caricature, he was a snake wearing a suit. He was on the front page of the newspaper, but I can hardly recall which newspaper it was and what words were written above the image. In a country in which more than ninety percent of the population were Christians, everyone could understand that radical Hutus were trying to dehumanize the leader of the RPA with this image and equate him to Satan, who, as a snake, was the devil responsible for the fall of man in the biblical story of Adam and Eve in the garden of Eden.

This snake imagery was undoubtedly referencing related stories that circulated about the Inkotanyi, or RPA soldiers, which alleged they were snakes or Avatar-like creatures that had tails and long ears, who were not human, let alone fellow countrymen. My friends and I almost believed these dehumanizing stories. Other stories were meant to convince Hutus of the animosity of Tutsis by telling stories of atrocities that the

RPA rebels allegedly committed in the Northern territory they controlled at the time. One of them was that they killed and tortured civilians, including babies, whom they allegedly killed by crushing them in wooden mortars with pestles.

One young boy from Byumba (an area in the Northern territory, then occupied by Tutsi rebels) stayed with us for a few months after fleeing the advance of the RPA and living in the Nyacyonga camp for internally displaced people. I still do not know how he left the camp and ended up in our village, which was in the southeast of the country, a trip that takes at least three hours by bus. Whether he walked all the way to our village, or traveled by bus, and where he had gotten bus fare in the latter case, remain a mystery to me. I do know that he was separated from his parents while fleeing the fighting and did not know their whereabouts, nor even whether they were still alive. He was a very sad boy, and I can never describe him well enough except to say that he wore dirty, ripped clothes and had an inconsolable face and a perpetually runny nose. He also had the appetite of a child who hadn't had enough food to eat for several months, and he wandered all over asking for food. He spoke with the northern accent of Kinyarwanda, which sounded funny to us. He was traumatized and used to isolate himself in the corner of our backyard and sing:

> Ni agahinda muri burende
>> (There is sadness in internally displaced people camps)
> Bararira cyane.
>> (There is a lot of tears.)

One morning we woke up, and he was gone.

The propaganda that contributed to tragedies like those that befell this boy came home to me one morning when I picked up a newspaper from my father's table. On the front page was a picture of a huge black mountain gorilla with a big nose. He had put both his fists in each of his nostrils. Above the picture read the warning that if you could not put at least three fingers into your nostril, you were not a real Hutu and you would not survive what was coming soon. It was a message from the far-right Hutu Supremacist political party, Coalition for the Defense of the Republic, CDR. The picture and the message petrified me. I was thin and tall, and I knew my nose did not have nostrils large enough to accommodate three fingers. I wished there was a surgical procedure to make my nose big enough to save me from the danger of having a small, long nose. But I was not going to give up. I was determined to live. My friends and I would quasi-surgically force two fingers into our nostrils several times each day to meet the standards we had seen on the front page of the newspaper.

I did not fully understand the seriousness of the message in the newspaper, but from what I saw on TV and heard about party meetings, I sensed that danger was probable. My aunt Théodosie was arrested and imprisoned the previous year for allegedly spying for the RPA and recruiting and teaching her students how to use a weapon before they joined the rebellion. When she was released, the prison guards shaved off all the hair on her head. This was enough to convince me that being associated with the Inyenzi, as they called RPA rebels, in any way was dangerous. The whole political drama was confusing to me, but I started understanding that some people in my country were in danger, and I could be one of them if I did not fix my nose.

Then at school one day, my best friend and classmate, Blaise, told me that there was going to be a full-blown war and that his family were going to fly away with Catholic nuns. I envied him for having nun friends who would take his family away to safety when the war intensified. I wondered how we would survive the war and how my friend knew it would reach us. Though I did not believe him entirely, part of me took him seriously. Anyone, even children, could see that war would escalate if the belligerents could not agree to share power.

The President Is Dead

It was April 1994. The news was everywhere. Everyone talked about it—the newspapers, radio, TV. "The president is dead!" they said. It felt like the world was ending. The country was decapitated. Radio Rwanda, the national radio network, played sorrowful classical music. The apocalypse was knocking at the door of our small, hilly country in the very heart of Africa. The official mourning period was announced. Everybody seemed worried and feared what was going to follow. Panic took control. Anti-Tutsi campaigns were all over the media. The interim government called on the population to "defend" themselves against the "invaders." The country was filled with a mixture of hysteria and confusion.

In my neighborhood, I was unaware of any killings happening for a few weeks, until one day my mother's goddaughter, Claudette, ran into our front yard, screaming and crying.

"They murdered my entire family!" she wailed.

Claudette's family lived only a few miles from our house, and she had miraculously escaped what was rumored to be an attack in retaliation against her father. Earlier, he had allegedly dug a deep hole in his backyard and drunkenly told people he was going to fill it with Hutus when the RPF won the war. According to other rumors, he dug the hole as a toilet but covered it and never used it. After his murder, I overheard older kids in the neighborhood say his body was thrown into that same hole. Whether the rumors about what he said were true, or whether they were a way to justify his death, I ignore them. He had the right to the benefit of the doubt, or to a fair trial if his words translated into criminal action. But at that time there were no trials, there were no judges, there was no benefit of the doubt; there was only chaos, and whoever had a machete and was Hutu was the judge.

In the 1959 uprising, when Tutsis were first killed and their houses burned in what was called by the Hutu government "the 1959 revolution," my mother and her family hid in the bush, feeding on raw papayas, and could not sleep in their houses for fear that they would be burned inside. She also recalled that those who found refuge in churches had survived. So, when Claudette arrived at our house, my mom took her, shaking with fear, into one of the rooms of our house. She was aware that killers were searching houses, and she told Claudette to leave through our backyard and go to the parish, about ten minutes walking distance from our house. She gave her one of her kitenge fabrics and a few clothes, walked her through the backyard down to the slope of the hill on which we lived, and wished her luck. We watched Claudette disappear into the banana plantation.

Tragically, the refuge found in churches in 1959 was not present in 1994. Tutsis who hid at the parish, including Claudette, were massacred there. They were killed even inside the Zaza Catholic church. The killers, who had gone to mass a few weeks before to pray, did not revere the church anymore. Temples were not sacred places anymore. In fact, nothing was sacred during that time. This still does not make sense to me.

It was like the biblical apocalypse in every way. Schools were looted. Windows and doors were broken. The girls' boarding school run by Abenebikira nuns, which my cousin Kayirere attended, was looted. One young man we knew passed by our front yard with about six mattresses on his head, which he had looted from the girls' school. We were standing at the front gate of our house and when he neared us, and my mother recognized him as her former student and asked him what he was going to do with all those mattresses. He replied that he would sleep on them all and experience how it felt to sleep on a mattress. The next day, when he went by our gate again to do more looting, we asked him how he felt and he said his back ached.

The country was in complete anarchy. Chaos was the law of the land. For a second, I wondered where the police were. What was the army doing? Where were the gendarmes? Where were the institutions of the republic? I wondered whether we would go back to school. I wondered whether we would also be killed. But we were not killed. Our turn had not come yet.

A few days later, as I played in the sweet potato field behind our backyard, I heard people screaming on the opposite hill by the parish eucalyptus forest. Two men were chasing a woman. Suddenly, the screaming stopped. The person that was being chased had been caught. The two men hunting her down were hacking her with what looked like machetes or some other tool that I could not recognize. I was terrified by what I saw, and I immediately ran back into our house, joined the rest of the family, and told no one what I'd seen.

About half an hour later, a girl came into our front yard. She was crying and carrying her younger sibling on her back. My mother and father recognized her. Her name was Sumwiza. Her family lived on the opposite hill from ours. She told us that her house had been attacked by killers who had murdered her family.

"The person I saw in the distance being murdered must have been a member of her family," I thought to myself.

Somehow, Sumwiza had escaped with her younger sibling, run down the hill from their house, crossed the valley that separated our hill and theirs, walked up the hill, and made it to our house. After she told my mother and father the story of how she had escaped, a story that we kids were not supposed to listen to, we heard a man shouting at our front gate. My father went to see who it was, and my sisters and I followed him. My father knew him. He lived a few miles from our house, by the path we took to fetch water at the public well situated on the edge of one of the many marshlands in the area. He had a machete that he was bumping onto the ground in anger, repeatedly. He looked like a lion ready to attack an antelope. Though he had not seen Sumwiza show up at our gate, he asked for her and sounded convinced that she was in our house, as if someone had told him her whereabouts. I wondered who among our neighbors would want such a young, innocent girl to be killed. My eight-year-old head could not wrap itself around the magnitude of the cruelty people were capable of unleashing onto others.

My father insisted that the girl had never come to our house. We all pretended that no one had seen a young girl carrying her younger sibling near our house. The man became even more furious. He threatened my father that he would face consequences for hiding Inyenzi. I did not understand how he could think that all Tutsi were RPA rebels, including kids. It was confusing. But I suddenly understood very clearly that my father was not a well-respected man in my village who had power and influence anymore; whoever had a machete and the backing of the genocidal provisional government was in charge.

My mother could hear the man talking from inside the house where she sat with Sumwiza and her sibling. Afraid that the killer would come search our house, my mother took the two children out through the backyard and told Sumwiza to go to the parish, as she had told Claudette. When she was sure the girl was far enough, my mother joined us at the gate. My father was firm about his decision not to let the man search our house. When the man realized that he was alone with no backup and could not attack our house without any proof that the girl was hiding there, he left angrily and promised we would regret what we had done.

Luckily, the man never came back to exact revenge on my family for refusing to cooperate with him. Three years after the genocide, I found out that Sumwiza and her sibling had survived. When we met, she was cordial to me, which I hoped meant she was thankful to my family. I never had the courage to ask her what happened to her after she left our house. I never asked her what she thought about my mother's choice to escort her out through the backyard so she could try to find refuge at the parish. I do not know what she went through after she left our house, but I thank God she survived.

The man who came chasing her was later convicted of genocide crimes and imprisoned. In 2010 I heard he was released. Though I did not have tangible proof that he killed anybody, I still wondered how he could be out of prison, living in the community with survivors. I wondered whether the sentence he served was long enough. I wonder still what I would say to him if I ever saw him again.

Horror Comes Home

My cousins Mzee, Dogori, and Safari lived in Kizihira, a small town that stretched from the parish and Zaza primary school. Their father, who had passed away a few years before the genocide, was believed to be Tutsi. Rumor had it that he had died of HIV/AIDS. One afternoon, soon after Sumwiza's sudden appearance at our home, my cousins showed up at our house unexpectedly. They were wearing banana leaves around their heads and waists like Hawaiian dancers in grass skirts. They also carried big sticks in their hands. I thought they looked cool, so I set about making myself a similar outfit without knowing that they had worn their strange costumes to disguise themselves as local militiamen and avoid being recognized and killed as they walked from their small village to our house. When they shared with us that they were being hunted down by their neighbors, my mother panicked and suggested we all go to my grandmother's house and die together as a family. But we did not leave our house. I suspect my father refused.

During this time, I overheard people saying that the leaders of the Interahamwe militia were unhappy that Hutus were not killing Tutsis in our sector. It was rumored that militias from the neighboring township of Kabirizi were going to come to our town and "do the work," as they called killing Tutsis. A few days later, it was not a rumor anymore. The militiamen attacked the parish and the seminary, where most Tutsis from the parish had sought refuge. They had hoped no one would dare attack the premises of the two Catholic institutions in the parish given the authority the church held in the area. But they were wrong.

Around 4:00 p.m. we heard noises of grenades and gunfire. A reddish, grayish, blackish smoke emerged on top of the parish forest from the direction of the seminary. It enveloped the sky with an apocalyptic smell of burning human flesh and property. A nightmarish twilight covered the sky of Zaza parish. I had never seen the sky like that before. Later hearsay had it that those who sought refuge in the seminary resisted the Interahamwe militiamen attacks, using stones and any objects they could find inside the confines of the Catholic school that prepared future priests. The nursery of future priests, as the bishop called it, had become a death factory. A crematory.

Mubande and Cyasa were two of the masterminds and killing machines who unleashed this hell on Tutsi civilians inside the seminary. They had returned from the Forces Armées Rwandaises (FAR) with grenades that they threw over the fence into the compound where the Tutsis hid. Unarmed, those hiding inside the school could not hold the fort. The degree of destruction of both human life and property was hellish. Five years later, when I started my secondary school at the Zaza Minor Seminary, the signs of the attack were still visible. Most buildings did not have any doors or windows on them. Corrugated iron sheets that once

covered the roofs were looted. Furniture and all school equipment were gone, too. Worst of all, smoke damage from burned
human flesh still covered the multipurpose hall, especially in the
basement of the building, where we held festivities on special
events like Saint Kizito Day, honoring the patron saint of the
school.

The family of my cousin Kennedy's girlfriend, Umwari, was
in the school when it was attacked by the ruthless killers. Her
father, who taught at the school, was killed there with his two
sons. His three daughters sneaked out of the building unnoticed with their little brother, Patrick, crossed the thick parish
forest, and found refuge with a family of friends who lived on the
outskirts of the forest. They stayed with them until the end of the
genocide. The little brother, who was five years old, then stayed
with my uncle, who lived a few hundred feet from our house.
This boy would later become my best friend in high school, in the
same seminary where his father had taught and been murdered
along with his two sons, five years before. I admired his courage
to carry on the family's scholastic legacy. He and his sisters knew
that their father would have wanted him, his only son who still
lived, to study in the school where he had taught.

After the genocide, I also found out that my friend Blaise and
his whole family had been exterminated by extremist Hutu militiamen. They never escaped with the nuns he'd said would help
them escape the war. I miss him very much and pray that his
soul rests in eternal peace. He was my closest friend at school,
and one of the smartest. His parents, like mine, were elemen-
tary school teachers. Blaise was right. Armageddon was immi-
nent. How I wish he and his family had made it to safety!

It seemed that even God had given up on the country of a
thousand hills, which legend held was His usual favorite place on

Earth to sleep at night. Clearly, He had spent the day elsewhere, and this time did not return to spend the night in Rwanda—at least not in our parish. Or maybe He slept in Rwanda but forgot to counsel the killers in their dreams to stop the carnage. Had God abandoned His people?

It's Time to Get Dressed

We had been hearing all kinds of gunfire from the distance for at least two days following my cousins' arrival at our house in their banana leaf costumes, and the attack on the seminary. The RPA was fighting the FAR at Rwamagana, which was about twenty-one miles from my village. On the third day, at sunset, my mother convened us in the backyard and said we had to leave our village. The fighting was just minutes away from us, and no one had any idea how long it would last. She told us to wear as many layers of clothes as we could, since we were going to walk and could only carry so much with us. As kids, we found that detail exciting, as it was fashionable to wear short pants inside our long pants. It even had a name: kugondeka.

At nightfall, we packed what we could and left home with our neighbors. We walked the whole night, up and down hills, crossing valley after valley. Finally, we arrived in a village where the grandparents of my friend Isaiah lived. Their house was surrounded by banana plantations on every side, except for a narrow alley that stretched from the road to the front door. I was tired and hungry from walking the whole evening. Our hosts spread mats in every space they could find in their tiny hut, and we sat down. The adults sat outside around a fire and were served banana wine. Women cooked plantains with peanut sauce in two big saucepans, enough to feed three families. When the meal was ready, they served it on two large plates and we sat in a circle around the food and ate with our hands.

Being used to eating with folks and spoons, I was at a disadvantage. The food was so hot that I could not touch it or swallow it like the other kids who shared my plate. By the time the food was cool enough for me to start eating, it was already gone and I had not eaten enough. My mother glanced at me with pity in her eyes. She was worried about me, but she could not do much about the situation, since we were staying with two other families and we had to share food. It would have looked bad if she had given me more food while other kids were not still eating. Afraid of creating misunderstanding with other mothers who stayed with us, she just called me to where she was sitting and told me that I had to learn to eat faster if I was to survive.

Growing up, we always had enough food in our house, so I never had to share a plate with other kids except on special occasions, like the naming ceremony of a newborn at our neighbor's house. Even then, I knew I would eat more at home, so I never worried about not getting enough food to eat. In fact, I did not know to sit still and eat, and I drank more than I ate. I would eat a few spoonfuls, play, and eat a few more, and play again until my plate was empty. I took my time since I had no competition. It often took me hours to finish my food, and most of the time my mother had to scold me so I would finish eating.

The next day, we left Isaiah's grandparents' house and camped with a few other families in the small town of Kirambo. More and more families came to our site, dragging their toddlers along, or carrying them on their shoulders, with mothers carrying the littlest ones on their backs with their kitenge or towels. By the evening of the second day, at least a hundred families had gathered in the small business center of Kirambo. The center was as noisy and crowded as an open market. Babies were crying everywhere. Toddlers were playing soccer on the dusty streets next to their mothers, who were cooking evening meals on open fires. Men were sitting on benches listening to Radio Rwanda and hoping to get any news of the status of the war, but the only thing the radio was broadcasting was doomsday gospel music by the Abasaruzi choir, alternating with the classical mourning music that had been on the air ever since the shooting of the presidential plane. The atmosphere was filled with despair and confusion.

The sun set and twilight fell upon Kirambo hill. I heard what sounded like a large group of people shouting as they approached the center where we camped. We went to see what was going on. A group of men with big sticks were pushing a young man in front of them while beating him with their sticks. The man was terrified and sweating. He was wearing nothing on his upper body, like Jesus being taken to Calvary to be crucified. His executioners said he was Inyenzi, or an RPA soldier. They also said he had scars on his shoulder and around his lower leg, which, according to them, meant he had carried a gun and worn military boots. They walked by the place where we camped, displaying and humiliating him as if to send the message that anyone among us who was spying for the RPA would face the same fate. I never found out what they did with that poor man, nor whether he was an RPA spy, but I have no doubt they killed him. One thing I do know is that no one deserves such treatment.

That same night, the center of Kirambo was flooded with many internally displaced people, so we moved to Kanazi, another hill next to Kirambo. We arrived on the slope of the hill cluttered with eucalyptus trees and ishinge, a type of green grass that people used to squeeze ripe bananas to make banana juice, and to sweep floors. We had no tents, nor any other material with which to build shelters. I wondered how we would sleep on the slope of the hill in the open, but I quickly realized that people become more creative in their most uncomfortable state. Men were already carrying eucalyptus trees they had cut from the edge of the hill to their families' respective sites. My cousins helped him construct a burende (a tent or tent-like shelter for refugees). While older children helped their fathers build shelters, younger ones helped their mothers find firewood to cook dinner. My mother boiled some sweet potatoes we had brought from home on a three-stoned open fire. Without enough firewood, the sweet potatoes were barely cooked, but we ate them anyway. We knew we could not expect to enjoy such luxuries as well-cooked meals in the situation we were in. By the time dinner was ready, our shelter was standing, but it was not well covered since the eucalyptus leaves my father used were not large enough to make a good roof.

After we ate, my mother spread her kitenge fabrics on the ground inside our "new home" and we all lay down to sleep. The light of the full moon penetrated the holes left in our shelter's roof by the tiny eucalyptus leaves. The uneven surface of the slope made sleeping uncomfortable, if not impossible. I barely slept that night. It was probably one of the longest nights of my entire life.

The Hill of Blood and Tears

By 5:00 a.m., everyone was up. Mothers were making porridge for breakfast, and kids were sitting around the fires, warming up their half-naked bodies. Men were busy looking for firewood. It seemed like a civilization was born on that hill after just one day. My ten-year-old sister, Lily, and my three-year-old brother, Valery, went to our uncle Thomas' shelter after breakfast, and my younger sister, Kiki, who was seven years old, followed them. I was with my cousin Kennedy at our shelter with my mother, father, and one-year-old brother, Thierry, eating the porridge that my mother had prepared for breakfast.

Suddenly, we heard gunfire right at the top of the hill. My mother grabbed Thierry and we ran to the bottom of the hill. Then we realized that Lily, Kiki, and Valery were not with us. My mother panicked and wanted to go back, but my father held her and calmed her down.

Then, a loud voice rose from the top of the hill: "Do not worry, we are here to protect you. There are a few Inyenzi coming up

37

from the other side of the hill, we would like to request help from some courageous men to fight them. Grab whatever weapon you have and come help us fight these cockroaches."

A group of men grabbed their bows and arrows and whatever weapons they could get their hands on and went up the hill to supposedly help fight the Inkotanyi. From where we were standing, we could see soldiers in combat uniforms with sneakers and different types of boots. They were wearing kitenge fabrics around their necks and waists. As we stood at the bottom of the hill watching men join these strangely dressed soldiers, Kennedy exclaimed in warning,

"These *are* Inkotanyi, look at their uniform!"

My father asked him whether he was sure of what he was saying, but I knew Kennedy knew what he was talking about. The RPA, or Inkotanyi, as we called them, wore a different kind of uniform than the National Army. It even had a name, Mukotanyi, to differentiate it from the regular uniforms. It was a grey and green mottled fabric, printed with brown, broken lines that looked like dry grass—a camouflage from when they fought in the northeastern savannah. Kennedy's mother and father were members of the Parti Libéral (PL), which was in the opposition alongside the RPF. He had gone with them to welcome the 600 RPA soldiers who had come to oversee the power-sharing process with President Habyarimana's regime, so he could recognize the difference between the Inkotanyi forces and the FAR (Forces Armées Rwandaises, or the National Army).

It did not take long to realize that what Kennedy was saying was true. As the men approached the soldiers on the top of the hill, the RPA soldiers started shooting at them. People screamed as they ran in all directions. Men, women, and children alike fell dead right in front of our eyes. My father called me to join him and my mother at the bottom of the hill, but my instinct told me to follow Kennedy, since he and I had always been inseparable. I ran towards him, across the hill, and towards a banana plantation on the edge of the hill. My father and mother kept calling after us to run to them so we could flee together, but it was too late.

Bullets were flying everywhere. As I ran in Kennedy's direction, I stopped short at an open pit, narrowly avoiding falling into it. A dead man had been thrown in there. He was wearing red pants and an orange t-shirt, his body swollen and starting to deteriorate. The pit was about seven feet deep. I went around it, bending down as low as I could to avoid flying bullets. I saw a woman carrying a baby on her back. She had been hit by a bullet, and her ear was bleeding, but she was still running with her crying baby wrapped on her back with a multicolored kitenge.

When I caught up with Kennedy, we both ran through a banana plantation. Even cows were afraid of the gunfire and were running with people in what looked like a nightmarish version of the Pamplona bull run. As we ran as far from the gunfire as we could, we recognized a man running in our direction. His name was Ndazivunye, and he lived in a small house on the path we took to my maternal grandmother's house or to the business center. (Kennedy and I also went by his house every day to buy my mother's Impala cigarettes at Ruhuteri's house. Ruhuteri's son, nicknamed Ninja, was the only seller of cigarettes and candy in the whole village. He started off buying and reselling one packet of cigarettes, and by 1994, he owned a wooden kiosk right across the street near my maternal grandmother's house— kwa Nyogokuru wo ku muhanda, as we used to call it.) Ndazivunye was not only familiar to us, and older, he serendipitously knew his way around the villages Kennedy and I were wandering.

He asked us to follow him, which we did.

I do not know where we would have ended up if we had not met Ndazivunye. He suggested that we go to my maternal grandfather's house, across Lake Mugesera. Neither Kennedy nor I had ever been there. Like many men of his generation, our grandfather had another wife besides our maternal grandmother. In fact, I had only ever seen him once at my maternal grandmother's house, which was a few miles from our house. The last time I'd seen him was when my uncle Mugenzi, who lived in Kigali, had come to visit with his whole family. Everybody on my mother's side was there on that weekend. We carried our mattresses to my grandmother's house, laid them in the living room and in every space that we could find in the house, and all lay down and slept. It was sort of like a family reunion.

I always loved when we all got together. There were at least fifteen grandchildren at my grandmother's house on those two days. It was in the summer and we were on the long school break, which went from June to September. We ate together from one big plate and played all sorts of games, from hide-and-seek to soccer. We bathed in the thick banana plantation behind my grandmother's backyard by the big jackfruit and passion fruit trees that seemed to coexist well with the tall green banana trees. We cut large banana leaves that we laid on the ground to cover the dirt, and we took cold baths using basins and buckets.

On the last day of my uncle's visit, he got into a fight with my grandfather. My grandmother had shared with him how my grandfather came to harvest bananas in her plantation even though he never helped to look after it. My grandfather's only defense was that everything my grandmother owned was truly his property, seeming to forget that he had a son, and that sons protect their mothers. Their long argument evolved into a fight in which my uncle Mugenzi stood and advanced towards his father to strangle him, but luckily my father held him back to prevent him from beating his father, which would have been a scandal in my culture. It was strictly prohibited to raise your hand on your parents, since they could curse you. My grandfather left without saying farewell and forgot his bike. Kennedy and I grabbed the bike and ran after him to return it to him.

So, when Ndazivunye mentioned that we were going to my grandfather's house, I wondered if he would welcome us. Our parents did not get along well with him after he left my grandmother, but we were still his grandchildren from his first marriage, and this was a matter of life and death. Gunfire noise sounded a little farther away from us, but we could still hear it distinctly, if not deafeningly so. I cannot describe how many kinds of gunfire noises I heard that morning. One sounded like a bunch of corrugated iron sheets hitting the ground. Others sounded like a combination of sharp, loud noises of birds in fast motion. We kept running, but this time not as fast, since we had to find a way to get to the shore of the lake.

Around noon, we arrived near the lake. We spotted a small hut a few hundred meters away and walked towards it. When we got close to it, Ndazivunye called out,

"Muraho abaha!" meaning, "Hello, residents of this home!"

Then a voice of an old man came from the hut, "Muri bande kandi murashaka iki?" ("Who are you and what do you want?") he asked.

Ndazivunye replied with relief that there was finally somebody who could help us cross the lake, "Turashaka kwambuka tukajya i Gatare." ("We would like to cross the lake to Gatare.")

The old man walked out of the grass-thatched hut, doddering with a walking stick in his right hand, and puffing his pipe. His neck bent forward because of age, he wore a wrap around his waist and nothing on his upper body, like a Rwandan Gandhi. "It's too dangerous to be on water!" he said. "You want to get us killed?"

Ndazivunye begged him to help us cross over to Gatare, and after long negotiations, which included handing him three bills of 100 Rwandan francs each, he agreed to transport us across the lake at nightfall. Then, he signaled us to enter his humble dwelling and wait there.

The entrance was narrow and low. We followed him inside and sat around the fire that he had kindled in the center of the hut. The suffocating smell of his pipe tobacco filled the single room, and I had to fight the urge to cough, lest someone hear us. A hammock-like bed was suspended in the right corner of the room, about four feet high, with a wooden ladder serving as stairs.

We waited for hours staring at each other. We did not want to speak for fear the soldiers could be nearby and hear us. The old man went out every now and then to make sure there was no danger approaching our hiding place. (We would later learn that the soldiers had followed a group of the Kanazi survivors who fled in the direction of Bugesera, a town that borders Burundi.) As the sun set behind the hills across the lake in the horizon, with its yellowish-red rays reflecting on Lake Mugesera, the time to cross over to Gatare was approaching. We helped the old man pull his canoe to the shore of the lake, and at twilight we stepped into the canoe and paddled across the lake. The canoe was long and narrow, and I wondered what would happen if a storm came our way. But the water was still, as if unbothered by the recent carnage. Our only fear was that soldiers could spot us and shoot at us, but fortunately, we made it safely ashore.

A group of men who stood on the shore of the lake quickly recognized the old man. We told them what had transpired that morning on the other side of Lake Mugesera and asked for directions to my grandfather's house. Fortunately, one of the men knew him well and could tell us the way. We walked up the hill and when we reached the main road, Ndazivunye wished us luck and went his way to his parents-in-law's home. Kennedy and I went with our guide, who led us to our grandfather's house, walking for at least an hour.

It was full moon and our shadows were distinct, like guardian angels walking by our sides. My cousin Mapua, whom I had not met before, was standing in the front door staring at passersby going to and from the business center to run the last errands of day and to have banana beer at the local bars. When she saw us, she walked into the house to call her mother, my aunt Abimana. Neither Kennedy nor I had met her before, so we greeted her and introduced ourselves, and she let us in. She called to our grandfather, who was in the backyard milking cows, and he came and hugged us. We gave him an account of how we survived the raid by the RPA and how we were separated from my parents and siblings. After we narrated the whole story, Abimana offered us some buttermilk and dinner was served. We had boiled sweet potatoes and kidney beans cooked in homemade butter. We were exhausted, both physically and emotionally, so right after dinner, Abimana made our beds and we went to sleep.

My grandfather's house stood on the edge of the Karisizo business center that stretched along the main road and was comprised of convenience stores and locally brewed banana beer bars, coexisting harmoniously. Like most of the houses in the banana-growing southeastern region of the country, it was surrounded by banana trees on all sides except the front. It was covered with a corrugated tin roof, like many houses in the area, with walls painted in white and brown ochre on the outside and decorated in black and white spiral imigongo (a form of art that uses color paint made from soil pigments, over a thick cow dung overcoat). The ceiling was made of thin bamboo sticks woven with red and plastic blue threads, and the floor was paved with a mixture of mud and cow dung.

In the backyard, cowsheds formed a natural fence and merged with imihata, the bamboo-like trees that are used to make fences. Next to the cowshed stood a kitchen covered with thatched grass, where Abimana made the family's meals. Abimana also made butter by churning kefir inside a big gourd, her back against the wall, her legs stretched out in front of her as she rocked the gourd of milk side to side until the butter separated from the milk. My grandfather always listened to Muhabura Radio, the radio station that aired RPF propaganda and my favorite Kayirebwa songs.

From my aunt Abimana we learned that she had not heard from her two sons in two months. They lived with her mother in Sake. Abimana decided to go find them despite the ongoing war. She asked Kennedy to accompany her, and they hit the road on foot since there were no cars or buses. There were also no mobile or public phones at that time, and very few people had landline phones. There was no way to communicate with our two dear pilgrims. Two days passed, then a week, then two weeks, and still we did not hear from them. My little cousin Mapua cried every night that passed without seeing her mother, and my grandfather was also worried. We started wondering if they had been intercepted on their way to Sake and killed by who-knows-who. I could not get used to the idea that I might not see Kennedy again. He was my best friend, protector, and the cool, city-hipster cousin who educated me about all the latest trends in music and fashion, and whom I boasted about to my friends.

As I worried about him, I recalled how I had always looked forward to going to Kigali with Kennedy for every school break. I could not wait for the trimester to end. I enjoyed not only my stay in Kigali with all the attractions the city had to offer a country child, but also traveling in a car, watching the trees alongside the road move in the opposite direction. I enjoyed everything from concerts, breakfasts, and new clothes, to sitting toilets. But most of all, I loved playing on the lit streets at night, and having electricity at home—a luxury I did not have in my village.

During the school year, Kennedy's father, my uncle Mugenzi, sent his kids to my village to stay with either my family or my aunt Theodosie's family so they could attend the schools where my mother and my aunt taught. This way, my mother would keep an eye on them and ensure they were taking school seriously, away from the city's distractions. Plus, they could get academic support from my mother, my father, and my aunt, who were all teachers. It was a family tradition, and before Kennedy, my cousin Jean de Dieu had also stayed with us until he went to secondary school.

Kennedy was about three years older than me, and the coolest boy in my town, if not the entire district. His fame partly came from the fact that he was from the city, but also from his incredible ability to attract people. He was funny, silly, and very likable. He was a good dancer and acrobat. He had a powerful influence on me and I emulated everything he did and was, good and bad. He introduced me to American R&B and funk music, and he taught me how to dance to the MC Hammer song, "U Can't Touch This." When he missed his girlfriend, he sang his favorite song, "Nothing's Gonna Change My Love for You" by

Glenn Medeiros. At that time, not many people in Rwanda spoke English, and I did not know a word of the language, but I loved the melody of this song. I was a child, but I felt the energy of the message in the tone of his voice.

Kennedy's sister, Kayitesi, also stayed with my aunt, but she returned home before the genocide broke out. For some reason, Kennedy was still with us when the violence started and could not travel to Kigali amidst the carnage. And now he was missing. Just like the title of the Medeiros song, nothing could change the brotherly love I had for Kennedy, and I feared for his safety.

I was still playful while at our grandfather's house, but my heart was heavy with sorrow caused by the possibility that my whole family could be dead. And now Kennedy, the only family I knew I had left, was also gone. We were starting to lose hope of ever seeing him and Abimana again. My stomach was tight with fear. Death was at every corner of the street I played on, at the lake where we went to fetch water, but somehow I felt I would survive. I considered all possible ways danger could come and engineered all sorts of plans in my head about how I would escape. How childish!

One evening, I saw a man named Rutayisire at the Karisizo Business Center. He had been my substitute teacher a few months before the genocide, when my mother was on maternity leave for my brother Thierry. We both recognized each other, and he asked me what I was doing in Gatare. I told him how I had been separated from my family and ended up in Gatare at my grandfather's house. At that point, Gatare had not suffered any attacks. Rutayisire was carrying a long gun, and he told me he was an RPF cadre. I decided not to ask him what he was doing at the business center near my grandfather's house. The same night I saw Rutayisire, people fled to the marshes on the shores of Lake

Mugesera to hide. But my grandfather refused to leave his house and said the RPF would not hurt him. He was listening to Radio Muhabura singing "Turaje ibihumbi n'ibihumbi, turaje we..." a popular nostalgic song about the return of Inkotanyi to Rwanda.

Face to Face with Death

My grandfather's house was as quiet as a tomb. Kennedy and Abimana were still not back, and we had not heard from them for weeks. My grandfather finished milking the cows, and then cooked my favorite beans with butter, which we ate with boiled sweet potatoes topped with kefir. He was very quiet and did not have much to talk about with me and my three-year-old cousin, Mapua, who was weeping and asking when her mother would come back. The mood in the house was not the same without Abimana and Kennedy. I went to bed with a tight stomach. I still did not know where my parents and siblings were, nor whether they were safe or dead.

In addition to being fearful, I was confused. I did not know why there was violence around me and why I was unsafe. I was eight years old and did not support any party in the conflict, nor did I understand why they were fighting. All I knew was that the president had died, and people started killing those who identified as Tutsis, and looting and burning schools. I also heard that

RPA rebels were fighting the government and that they were killing people, too. I could not quite connect all the dots; neither could I find out what side I was supposed to be on, nor whom I should be fearing.

"What am I, and who wants to kill people who look like me?" I constantly wondered. "How do they recognize them, and why do they want them dead?" From the newspapers I read, I knew my nose did not qualify me as a real Hutu, but I was not attacked when Tutsis were hunted down.

My aunt Théodosie had been jailed because she allegedly spied for the RPF, but now the RPF was attacking us. I went to bed confused, terrified, and sorrowful. I missed my family. I missed Kennedy. I sensed death everywhere, and I was determined to stay alive. It had been a long day, and I was tired. I quickly got carried away by the thoughts and fell into a deep sleep.

Then suddenly I heard a voice calling me by the nickname that everybody called me, Petit: "Petit, Petit—byuka wumve!" (Wake up!)

I suddenly awoke, as if from death, and asked, "Ni iki, ni iki?" (What's happening?)

My grandfather said, "Sh sh sh! Ceceka!" (Keep quiet!)

Then I heard people marching in front of the house on the main road.

My grandfather's house was just a few feet from the main road. At first, it sounded like herds of cows walking by, but it was too early to take cows for grazing, and no one in town had a herd big enough to make such a sound. Then, the sound became clearer and clearer. It was the sound of boots, and they produced a rhythmic, thunderous sound, like King Kong marching into the streets of New York City. I followed my grandfather to the window in the living room. We carefully pulled the curtain back about three inches to see who it was. My eyes set on a crowd of men in military uniform holding their AK-47s and marching past my grandfather's house as if in a parade.

It was about 4:45 in the morning and the sky was still a little dark. The men were quiet except for the rhythmic sound of their boots hitting the dirt ground. They were wearing the same uniform Kennedy had recognized at Kanazi as belonging to the RPA rebels, the material with markings that looked like bits of dry grass. I remembered how those men shot through the crowd of internally displaced people. Most of them were wearing caps that matched their uniforms, and others were wearing casual caps. Many were also wearing farm boots and sneakers, except for a few who wore military boots.

We stood by the window, petrified, and watched them for about half an hour as they walked in parallel, single-file lines past our house. They were heading down the road towards Lake Muge-sera in search of those who hid in the papyrus marshes on the shores. As soon as they disappeared in the distance, my grand-father woke up Mapua and told us to get out of the house. The previous night he had refused to hide, but now he looked terri-fied, and I understood we were in danger. I was thinking of all the ideas that could convince the men that I was on their side—that I owned the Parti Libéral (PL) cap, for example. Kennedy had told me his family had welcomed the RPA battalion at the parliament building as they came to supervise the power-sharing process. I thought I would mention that to them, and maybe they would understand that I wasn't their enemy.

We got out of the house and headed to the banana plantation that stretched right from the backyard. We sat there for at least ten hours. No one was talking. Even Mapua did not cry. The birds did not sing like they always did. When the sun arrived at its zenith, we were getting hungry, but my grandfather was afraid to return to the house and find some provisions, so we dug up cassava and sweet potatoes from a nearby field and ate them raw. I was thirsty, but I did not even bother asking for water. I could see there was no way to get anything from the house. But we did not hide. We sat between banana trees in the open, not knowing from which direction danger would come. My grandfather must have thought the soldiers would raid the marshes and go back through the main road. He was wrong. They were going to search all the bushes and find every living soul.

It was around 4:00 p.m., and we were still sitting in the shade of three banana trees that provided a natural shelter. Then suddenly, we heard people speaking Swahili walking in our direction. It was too late to run so we sat still and hid behind the banana trees. About ten soldiers walking in a horizontal line towards our location stopped and stood above us.

My grandfather hastened to say, "We are not your enemies."

The men who were closest to us said, "Come with us. We will take you to our commander and he will decide what to do with you."

We stood and walked in front of the soldiers as they pointed their guns at us, telling us where to go. Some of them spoke a language I did not understand that sounded like Swahili, but was not Swahili. It must have been Luganda or Lunyankole-Ruciga.

We arrived at a house that other soldiers were destroying. The soldiers told us to sit down. The commander was not there. In fact, I later realized they never had a plan to talk to their commander, and one of those very men might have been the commander of the platoon or section. We obeyed. My grandfather sat down first, and then I sat next to him, and Mapua sat next to me in a horizontal line.

My grandfather continued to beg them to spare our lives, repeating that we were innocent and supported their cause. Coldly, they told my grandfather to lie on his belly, but he kept imploring them to spare his life. The soldiers insisted that he lie on the ground, and that it was going to be quick. I was next in line, and where I sat, I was trembling with fear and reciting Our Father and Hail Mary prayers like my Catholic parents had taught me. Mapua was sitting next to me and did not seem to understand what was going on.

Then my grandfather obeyed and lay flat on his belly. At first I thought they were going to beat him and let us go. I never thought they would kill him. They seemed to be nice people and behaved very calmly and talked normally. But I was naïve. As soon as my grandfather lay down, two of the soldiers cold-bloodedly pulled the triggers on their guns and shot him simultaneously. I was sitting down, still praying and wondering whether I should run or keep sitting and wait to be killed. It all happened so quickly and unexpectedly. As they shot my grandfather, I jumped up and ran zigzagging in the opposite direction. Behind me, I heard Mapua cry as she sat and watched our grandfather get killed in front of her eyes. But I could not go back to get her. I kept running as fast and as far as I could.

When I could not hear anyone behind me, I stopped and sneaked into a small bush that I saw on my right, between two banana fields. I squatted there, hands and feet numb, out of breath from running, as hungry and thirsty as I could possibly be, but I did not move lest anyone hear me and come to kill me. I was frozen with fear. Almost paralyzed.

I remained in a state of shock for almost an hour or so and was not able to feel my body. It seemed almost like I was a hollow skeleton with breath blowing through the large, empty spaces between bones. My spirit almost traveled to another dimension. My physical self stopped living for hours, and I could only feel my spirit flowing in an empty space, thinking about nothing at all, in a state of utmost nothingness.

When I came back to physical reality, my hands and feet hurt. I changed my position and sat on my bottom, relaxed my hands and feet in the tiny space that I occupied, and replayed the scenes I had lived a few hours earlier. I wondered whether they had spared Mapua's life since she was only three years old and a girl. I had heard the many shots fired at my grandfather, so I had no hope that he miraculously survived.

I stayed in the bush the whole night, changing body postures every now and then. I did not sleep or drift off for a second. The night was as quiet as a grave. I felt neither pain nor cold. No animals come out from hiding, nor did I hear birds sing. I did not hear or see any living soul the whole night, and I did not regret it. Human beings had become the new beasts, and animals were my least fear.

So much had happened in the previous hours that I lost all sense of time. Whether the night felt long or short, I had no idea. Once in a while during the night, I would change positions after the side against the ground numbed.

Dawn broke, and instead of feeling safe, I was frightened. For the first time, daylight scared me more than darkness. After carefully inspecting my surroundings to make sure the soldiers had left, I slowly came out of my hiding place, tiptoeing through the banana plantation, avoiding the dry banana leaves that covered the ground, lest they crack and draw the attention of anyone who could hurt me.

I arrived near my grandfather's house and was welcomed by an inauspicious scene of smoking houses. What had been an inhabited village the day before was now desolate. The neighbors' houses I visited a few days earlier were all burning. The playground I played on the day before was a desert. For a moment, I wondered whether I was the only person to survive the apocalypse. I was alone, walking through houses and banana trees. The air was heavy with smoke, and I walked through like a hungry, bony, zombie child emerging from the dead. My lips were parched. No birds sang. No dogs barked.

The silence around me was deadly. The only noise I could hear came from my terrified mind, and the only living people I saw were in the recalled scenes of the last people I had seen the previous day. I replayed them over and over in my traumatized mind: my grandfather being shot, my cousin sitting next to me, the tall, slender soldiers who had physical features similar to mine, and who almost killed me as though we had nothing in common, not even our humanity. They killed my grandfather in cold blood and seemed utterly phlegmatic about their ignoble act. I asked myself what we had done to deserve death. I wondered what I, an eight-year-old, naïve boy who did not know even the least thing about the conflict, had done to endure such carnage.

The previous year, my friends and I had attempted our natural "plastic surgery" to make our noses larger. I wondered whether my nose had not enlarged enough. But my grandfather had a bigger and shorter nose than I, and so did my little cousin, Mapua. Had they been killed because they had bigger and shorter noses? Did I have to reverse my plastic surgery and make my nose longer and thinner? Clearly, the game had changed, so if I wanted to survive I would have to adapt. From that time, I told myself I would massage my nose every now and then, by pressing it from the eyes downwards, compressing the nostrils so they would appear small. Even today, I catch myself unconsciously touching my nose, massaging it as if to make it longer and smaller.

Having a short nose was not a physical trait that was regarded as attractive. My cousin's Mapua's name was a nickname given to any child in my mother's family who had a shorter nose than the average family member. In fact, my other cousin who also had a shorter nose had been given the same name and was often teased about it. Such nicknaming practices were not rooted in a failure to accept a child, but were rather a way to remind the child to be humble. In retrospect, I do see how such a nickname reveals beauty standards that were predetermined by the pre-colonial ruling Tutsi class and by subsequent colonial masters. Every child in the family had a part of the body that was not perfect per such beauty standards, so others picked on them to tease them, or to teach them to feel comfortable and embrace their imperfections. I was singled out for my big ears. Even if everybody in my family had big ears, I had the biggest, maybe because I was very thin, which amplified their size, and I did not grow long hair to cover them. But having big ears was not something that was regarded as unattractive in the same way that having a short nose was. I earned the nickname Matwi (Big-ears), and my closest friends picked on me about the size of my ears; but I had a lot of pride in them and had learned to say my big ears meant that I was a better listener.

When dehumanizing propaganda about RPF soldiers described them as having big ears, and tails, I did start to become self-conscious. I felt ashamed and feared that I might be profiled as Inkotanyi or Inyenzi (RPF fighters), which was dangerous at that time. Later, when the RPF won the war, I felt some pride in that stereotype. I liked the fact that I had big ears like the victors of the war.

But this stereotypical feature did not save my life the day my grandfather was murdered in front of my eyes...or maybe it did. I couldn't be sure. As I walked in the now barren village, lost in my thoughts, I wondered why the soldiers who assassinated my grandfather had not followed me or shot at me as I jumped and ran away. Would they have spared my life had I stayed sitting there? Did they not shoot at me as I ran away because I did not look Hutu? These are the questions I will probably never find answers for.

When I later learned that they had killed my three-year-old cousin after I ran away, I had no other reason to believe that they might have spared my life. "But my cousin, even if she was very young, she had a short nose," I thought.

Did they kill her because she fitted the stereotype of a Hutu? How did the soldiers decide who would live and who would die? Or did they kill anyone they came across? Until today, I have not been able to understand their motives, the orders they received, nor from whom.

I reached the outskirts of Karisizo business center as I pondered all these questions without any breakthrough. I had not come across any sign of life so far.

Then I heard a voice coming from behind a house on my left, "Bite?" (How's it going?)

I startled.

The man calling me did not wear a military uniform, so I cautiously hoped he might not hurt me. He did not seem threatening and did not have a weapon with him. After scrutinizing him, I responded,

"Ni byiza," (I'm doing well)

But I wasn't doing well. I had escaped death by a few inches and watched my grandfather, the only family member I knew was alive, get murdered. I had run away, leaving my cousin behind, failing to save her life. I was hungry and thirsty, and for the past twenty-four hours I had not drunk any water and was dehydrated. The only thing I had eaten was raw cassava. But my biggest worry was finding someone who would take me with them to safety, whatever that meant.

The young man, who might have been in his early twenties, asked me where I was from. I told him the whole story of how I had ended up in Gatare after I was separated from my family; how my grandfather had been killed the day before; and how I did not have anywhere else to go, since I did not know anyone in the village. When I mentioned my grandfather's name, he said he remembered hearing about the grandchildren from Karembo, and he realized that I was one of them. Everybody knew everybody, and my arrival in the town with Kennedy had not gone unnoticed by the dwellers. I spent that morning with this young man, who later heard that Godereva, my grandmother's cousin who also lived on the same hill, was asking for me. I had seen her once and barely remembered that we were related.

The man took me to Godereva's house. She was overjoyed to see me and gave me the biggest hug with her long arms. She was about six-feet, four-inches tall, but she walked with her back bent forward from age. She asked how I had survived and I told her the whole story of how I witnessed my grandfather get killed, and how I miraculously escaped the killers. She was overflowing with empathy and gratitude. After she listened to my story, weeping and fixing me with her weak but compassionate eyes, she gave me a bench to sit on, and without asking whether I was hungry or thirsty, she brought me some banana juice in a calabash. She also brought me leftover beans and sweet potatoes, which I devoured like a hungry lion, without caring about any of the strict table-manners my mother had martially inculcated in me.

I had not taken a shower for many days, and my body was sore and bruised from running and crawling through the bushes. I had not run away with spare clothes, and after Abimana left, my grandfather did not remind me to wash them, so I had worn the same outfit for at least three months and had taken only a handful of showers. Godereva gave me the longest and most punctilious bath. In that village, no one had a modern bathroom or running water in the house. Children were bathed outside standing on banana leaves carefully laid on the ground in the backyard. Bathing water was put in a bucket or a big plastic bowl or basin. Godereva scooped water from the bucket, wetted me, and scrubbed me with a luffa scrubber soaked in water and soap. After my skin dried in the sun, she smeared my whole body with homemade butter and massaged me with her big strong motherly hands, hardened by decades of plowing fields and doing the many chores that women were expected to do in our patriarchal society.

After a few days of smearing butter on my body before going to bed, all the rashes disappeared and my skin rejuvenated. I spent a few weeks with Godereva, and for the most part, the village was peaceful. I became friends with her grandchildren, whom I would accompany to Lake Mugesera to fetch water. They taught me how to catch fish and how to find bait in the marshes, but Godereva had made it clear to them that I was not supposed to swim in the lake, lest I drown and die. I was the only person from my family that she knew was alive, and she wanted to make sure I would live to tell the story, and most importantly, to procreate and revive the family. In Rwanda, even today, it is considered the number one responsibility of a son, especially the eldest son, to expand the family, continue the legacy of his father, and ensure the family genes are passed on. At that point, we did not know the whereabouts of my siblings or parents, nor whether they were still alive.

Rain of Bullets

I spent my days playing with Godereva's grandchildren, and after dinner I would go to sleep at her house with one of the grandchildren. After a week passed, we heard there were going to be more attacks on our village. People started preparing for places to hide. There was no other place to go that would provide safety for the villagers, so people decided to go live in the papyrus marshes of Lake Mugesera. We established a settlement in the middle of the marshland, halfway from water and land. People cut papyrus trees and built shelters. Some shelters were bigger and had rooms. Depending on the tide, the surface was wet, and walking through the marshes was difficult, as one had to jump over big holes filled with water. Everyone had deserted their houses and only returned there at night to cook.

Somehow the villagers gathered intelligence and learned precisely when the next attack would be launched on the village. We spent the night in our papyrus-made shelters. It was cold and wet. Everyone had been briefed not to cook lest the soldiers see the smoke and find out where we hid.

The next morning, as soon as dawn broke through the thick papyrus forest and the sun shone on the still water of Lake Mugesera, we heard the first gunshot from the hill. Everybody woke up in a panic, and before I could walk to the next shelter to find Godereva's sons, I heard more deafening gunshots. As I prepared to jump and run, a strong hand grabbed me and pushed me to the wet surface. Then a voice said,

"Lie down or you'll be shot at."

The speaker was a strong, large lady who must have been in her thirties. I did not know her, but I did not care. It was very dangerous to walk through the marshes, and many people were stuck or sank into the many holes that spread around the surface. It was hard to know which direction the shots came from, or to guess which direction was safe to move in, but this lady held my hand and crawled with me as far from the land as possible. The journey was perilous, and we fell into swampy water holes multiple times. Each time, she pulled us out and we continued to crawl and run in between gunshots. The closer we got to the lake, the more water holes we encountered. Sometimes she put me on her back and jumped large ditches of water like Wonder Woman.

We arrived at a place where we could see the lake and people across the lake in Kizihira, at the popular paper mill, or Papeterie as it is locally referred to, on the shore of Lake Mugesera. We stood mired in black, swampy mud that came up to my knees for hours, our ears deafened by the thunderous, heavy gunshots that fell on the papyrus trees like the stormy Umuhindo (first rainy season from September to December) rain on ceiling-less tin roofs. The whole day, we ceaselessly heard a mixture of people screaming and gunfire, as we stood shaking with fear and cold, without speaking to each other.

As the sun began to set, the gunfire stopped, but we did not move for a while. Eventually, we started heading back towards the hillside, following the footprints we left earlier. As we approached the edge of the marshland with fewer and shorter papyrus trees, we started meeting people coming out of hiding and we saw other people reach the foot of the hill. We walked through the crowd of women wearing multicolored kitenge fabrics, with their babies strapped on their backs with more kitenge fabrics or bath towels, and holding the hands of their older offspring, some of them crying, asking for food.

Men were beginning to look around for food at nearby farms, and the brave ones went as far as their houses to retrieve provisions. Young men went to the lake to catch fish for dinner and women kindled fire and breastfed their crying, terrified, hungry babies. We hastened through the crowd asking whomever we came across whether they had seen Godereva, her grandchildren, or her sons. As we walked, we also met other children, women, and men looking for their loved ones. We stumbled upon a mother and her son whom I had seen at Godereva's house. They recognized me and informed us that Godereva was alive. They took me to where she sat cooking dinner, and she hugged me so tightly that my weak body hurt. She looked me in the eyes and hugged me again, this time longer.

"Imana ishimwe!" (Thank God!) she cried. "Imana yumvise amasengesho yanjye!" (God heard my prayers!)

She then thanked the young lady who had selflessly and bravely carried me on her strong back and taken me under her protection as we fled the shelling.

Nightfall covered the hill of Gatare, and the last rays of the setting sun disappeared over the horizon. It was too late to harvest sweet potatoes or cassava, and it was dangerous to go back to the house to get cassava flour to make ubugali (foufou). One of Godereva's grandsons went to the banana plantation and harvested a bunch of plantains that were not well plumped up. When he brought them, we realized that they were not the type that you cook, but the ones you make juice from. But we had no other choice, so we boiled them and ate them with freshly caught fish. The plantains were bitter and almost impossible to swallow, but we had nothing else to eat and we were hungry, so we ate them anyway. This reminded me of a proverb my mother used to repeat to us whenever we said food was not tasty, "Haryoha inzara," meaning when you're hungry, anything is tasty. Before the genocide and war, I had never eaten something I did not like because I was hungry or because I had to—except the vegetables and peas my mother made sure I grew to like. Food was plentiful at home.

After eating our humble dinner, we lay on the bare surface of the banana plantation, at the foot of the hill, and slept. I was very tired, so I drowsed for a few hours. The surface I slept on was uneven and uncomfortable. I only covered myself with a light-weight kitenge. I had not had time to process what I had been through that day, so as soon as I lay down, I began to replay the scenes.

Not many people died that day, only those who had not left their homes, and a few unlucky ones who were close to the edge of the marshland. The soldiers had not advanced farther into the papyrus-covered marshes for fear that some people might have weapons. Instead, they stayed on the outlying parts of the marshes and shelled through the papyrus trees. Nevertheless, I thought, "I would have been killed or trodden upon by fleeing people if it wasn't for the young lady who grabbed my arm from nowhere and ran with me away from the gunshots."

This was the third attack I had survived since the beginning of the war. This young woman had saved my life, and I did not even know her name. She could have run away by herself, which would have been faster, but she did not do so. Why did she act more humanely toward me than the soldiers who killed my grandfather and my three-year-old cousin? How did she develop these heroic instincts? She did not have time to make the decision whether she should save me or not, and yet she did. What did she see in me? Did she see something in common with me? Was she my guardian angel, like the priests had taught me? I did not know of any female angels. Angels had male names like Michael and Gabriel. Could I have a female guardian angel even if I was male? I did not have an answer to that question.

I wondered whether my siblings and parents were dead or alive and whether my friends Isaiah and Kizito had survived or not. I wondered whether the war would ever be over and whether I would see my friends again. Darkness enveloped the sky but frogs did not stop croaking from the marshes, as if singing mourning songs for those who had perished from the killings that day. I drifted off through the sad grating noise of the frogs into a deep sleep.

The next morning, I awoke to the sound of mothers making porridge and washing saucepans. We returned to Godereva's house and she fixed her usual porridge with a mixture of corn, cassava, sorghum, and soy flour. Routines resumed as if nothing had happened, but we lived in constant fear of the next attack. Stories of raids on neighboring hills circulated by word of mouth. We heard that a hill not far from where we camped was attacked, and this time the soldiers released prisoners from all the jails situated in the areas they had conquered. The prisoners then advanced through the marshes with short axes and other traditional weapons, killing everyone who hid there. As the news spread, people started to realize that there was no place to hide. I overheard Godereva's older son tell her he was mapping out a strategy to flee to Tanzania.

Reunion with Lily and Valery

It was a morning like any other. I was playing soccer with Godereva's neighbors' kids in the front yard. As I went to pick up the ball that my friend had kicked across the road, I saw two people walking toward me, but I did not recognize them. I picked up the handmade plastic-bag soccer ball, crossed the road again, and as I kicked it to my friend, I heard a voice call out to me from behind, "Petit!"

I turned around, and saw my sister Lily with Francisca, the wife of my oldest uncle, walking towards me. I stood there and stared at them in disbelief as they approached me, as if I had seen ghosts. Then my sister said, "Petit, it's us."

I had recognized them by then, but I was just in shock because I had not imagined them alive, and I did not know how to react. I stood still and looked at them as though they were revenants. My sister walked to me and hugged me, and Francisca did the same. I remained silent, unsure of how to respond. They asked me where Godereva was, and I escorted them to the backyard, where she sat peeling sweet potatoes.

Then Francisca greeted her, "Muraho Godere."

Godereva stared at them and burst in tears. "Is that you, Francisca?" she cried. They hugged for the longest period, and when they were done, she offered them banana juice and attended to them like the culture required.

We shared stories of how we had survived. My sister and I had separated on Kanazi hill when the RPA soldiers shot through the camp in which we had spent the night. She fled with my younger brother, Valery, who was three at that time. They wandered around, hiding in bushes until they finally came across RPA soldiers who questioned them about their identity and provenance. In this conundrum, who you knew or were related to could save you or get you killed. My sister, who was ten years old at the time, understood this, so she lied about their identity and told the soldiers they were related to a young, wealthy Tutsi couple that had been killed by Interahamwe militia from Kabirizi. The soldiers believed her, and took her and Valery to a camp of internally displaced people that was set up in schools and stores in the town of Zaza. Lily and Valery happened to have the most stereotypically Tutsi features in our family. They were both tall with fine facial features and long noses. I wondered whether the RPA soldiers would have believed such a statement from my younger sister, Kiki, who looked the least Tutsi because she had inherited a short nose from my mother's side of the family.

The night my sister and brother arrived at the camp in Zaza, they were placed in a classroom at the primary school where my mother was a teacher. There they met my cousin, Mutima (or rather, my sister, since in the Rwandan culture cousins from one's father's side are considered siblings, not cousins). Mutima had also been found by RPA soldiers with her nanny, Odetta, and they were brought to the transitional camp in Zaza. People did not go back to their homes until the RPA was sure that they had eliminated all the elements they deemed dangerous. Every night, the soldiers would go into the classrooms where they slept and take men, women, and older boys. No one knew where they took them. One day, they came and took Odetta, and Mutima never saw her again. When she asked a child soldier (Kadogo, as they were often called), he responded that they were killed and incinerated in the eucalyptus forest next to the seminary.

At that time, the 1994 genocide survivors and the Tutsi returnees who had fled in 1959 were still very resentful, and a lot of soldiers and civilians carried out revenge killings against Hutus. Many people who returned to their homes were killed or imprisoned by those who wanted to seize their property. Luckily, my sister, brother, and cousin were not killed; instead they received special treatment from soldiers who assumed they were kids who had survived the wrath of Interahamwe militia. They were both put under the guardianship of a genocide survivor and widow who took care of them until Francisca found them.

As for Francisca, she had ended up in Kibungo city. She was intercepted by RPA soldiers as she fled the fighting and was given the responsibility of looking after all the orphaned children. She had earned the name Bibi, which means grandmother in Swahili, the language that most RPA soldiers spoke in addition to Luganda and Kinyarwanda. When it was relatively safe for people to return to their homes, she returned to our village where she met my sister, my brother, and cousin. They stayed together at a neighbor's house that was closer to the main road and therefore considered safer than our house, which was farther away from the main road.

After Lily and Francisca had narrated the whole story of how they had all survived, they told me I was going to leave with them and return to our native town. I was so excited that I was going to finally see my brother Valery and other friends who had survived the killings. My sister and Francisca spent the night at Godereva's house, and early morning the next day, we hit the road. I was anxious to arrive, but I was also afraid of the journey itself. My cousin Kennedy and my aunt Abimana had not come back yet, so I did not know what we might encounter on our journey from Gatare to Karembo. My village was about a three-hour walk. But walking such a distance was no longer a painful experience for me. After months of running from hill to hill, crossing rivers and lakes, I was in good shape.

After bidding farewell to Godereva, we left. We went down and up the deserted hills and past empty houses. Bananas were ripening on their trees. Every now and then we would encounter the nauseating odor of decomposing human bodies, and we hurried to pass it as fast as we could. Dogs had lost guidance from their human masters. Human violence had brought up their wilder instincts, and they fed on human bodies.

We passed by desolate houses, abandoned by their owners who had fled the fighting. Francisca and Lily had not returned to our house to reoccupy it. Most people in our neighborhood had not returned to their houses. They stayed at Rehuteri's house so that they could be near the main road, closer to other people they knew. It was not yet safe to return to one's house. There was no market at that time, so when people needed food, they broke into abandoned houses and took all the food that was there, as well as other supplies they needed in their homes. It was called "kubohoza," meaning retrieving what had been stolen from you, in contrast with "gusahura," or looting. The latter was the term used to refer to pillaging by Interahamwe militia and some Hutus when they grabbed what belonged to Tutsis and looted public buildings including schools and hospitals.

In a way, there was a difference between the two types of stealing, but both were still looting, since people took what did not belong to them even when they did not know whether the owners would return. But kubohoza was authorized by the RPA soldiers. After order was reestablished, it was very common to go to someone's house and find one's furniture among their other belongings. Those who were kind would return things to their original owners, but most people kept what they had looted (kubohoza), including TV sets, bicycles, cars, and other home equipment. We knew who had taken our water filter but we did not bother asking for it.

We arrived at Rehuteri's house at sunset. I was overjoyed to see Valery. We stayed for about two weeks, and then one after-noon, Xaverine, my uncle's wife, arrived at our house. At that time, if someone's whereabouts were unknown, they were assumed to be dead, so every reunion was miraculous and surreal. Xaverine was coming to see if her son, my cousin Kennedy, had survived and what had happened to everyone from my family. She was devastated to hear from me that Kennedy had left our grandfather's house with Abimana and never returned. My sister Lily, my brother Valery, and myself were the only people from my family who were known to be alive at that time, and by cultural obligation, my uncle had the responsibility to take us under his custody as his sister's children. Xaverine stayed for one night and informed us that we would leave with her to go to my uncle's house in Kigali. I was very excited at the idea, since I had always been fascinated by city life.

At My Uncle's in Kigali

The next morning, we packed our humble belongings and walked to Zaza to find a ride to Kigali. At that time, there were no buses, and no transportation services worked. Our plan was to hitchhike to Kigali. Zaza was a small, parochial town with three Catholic secondary schools, one private secondary school that my father had helped found, two primary schools, and a health center. All of these places revolved around the Catholic parish of Zaza, which was the second-oldest parish, after Save, established by White Fathers in 1902. It was where I went to school and to mass every Sunday, but it was rendered almost unrecognizable after the genocide and war.

As mentioned earlier, all three secondary schools had been looted and the seminary burned down by Interahamwe militia who faced resistance from Tutsis hidden inside the school. The Ecole Normale de Zaza, the teacher training school my father attended (and where I went every Sunday to watch a handball game, animated by commentators and DJs playing the latest

R&B and Zook music) was transformed into a temporary military barrack. CLAC, the cultural center where I went to watch black-and-white movies on our family outings and play with the rare western toys that the kids' section offered, had been looted and did not look like it had ever been operational. The beautiful gardens of flowers and lawns that used to be well cared for and trimmed by parishioners on a regular basis had been invaded by wild bushes that covered them and climbed up to the walls of the parish. The girls' school run by Abenebikira nuns, Lycée de Zaza, had been looted, including the mattresses that once provided sleeping comfort that many girls did not have in their humble homes.

The Zaza I saw did not look like the heart of the Mugesera District's civilization that it had been just a few months before. It was not the place I looked forward to visiting for school, mass, or to see my friends who were children of secondary school teachers at their beautiful homes provided by the schools. The streets had not been swept for months by the many women who once took a lot of pride in keeping their parish spotless.

The beautiful, gothic-style church that had been a place for worship and communion between God and the parishioners had become a tomb, or rather a slaughterhouse. Tutsis who had taken refuge there were brutally slain, even at the very altar where the killers and killed alike had received communion and prostrated in reverence of Christ, who they believed was present in the Tabernacle hung in the right corner of the altar.

People were murdered even in the Zaza Health Center, where I was born and took my first vaccines. What was once the hub of spirituality, education, health, and culture for nearby and faraway people had become a mass grave in which everything that had once given life to the town was buried. In just four

74

months we had descended from heaven to hell. I wondered what God must be thinking about the human species that scriptures said was His/Her/Its proudest creation. I wondered whether God regretted creating human beings. I did not have any answer to this question, and the idea of God became even more confusing to me than it had ever been before. The priests, in their homilies (which my mother instructed me to listen to carefully), had mentioned that God was all powerful, and that God loved us so much that God had sent His/Her/Its only son to save us. But God did not save my countrymen. God did not save my grandfather, or my little cousin Mapua.

"Either God is Almighty but did not care for His/Her/Its people, or God is not Almighty at all," I thought.

We waited along the main road and hitchhiked every car that passed by to request a ride to Kigali. Most of the cars were driven by soldiers. Others were trucks full of 1959 Tutsi refugees who were returning to Rwanda from neighboring countries. Most of them spoke Kirundi or Kiswahili because they had lived in Burundi for many years. In fact, they called those of us who had been living in Rwanda, Rwandans, and people called them Abarundi or Burundians to refer to the Burundian diaspora. Their culture was somewhat different from the people who had grown up in Rwanda; even their culinary preferences were slightly different.

After waving at dozens of cars that passed by, we found a truck that was going to Gashora, which is about halfway to Kigali and is near the tarmac road. There would be more traffic there, and hence a better chance to find a ride to Kigali. The driver agreed to give us a ride up to Gashora, where we would stop and find another ride to Kigali. We climbed in the back of the big truck and we took off. The road was bumpy and dusty. It was the beginning of the summer, and it was very hot in the back where we sat in the truck bed, its back side open.

Gashora is about an hour drive from Zaza, but the drive felt longer partly because I was impatient to arrive at our destination, and because of the grueling ride on the rutted dirt road. My brother Valery, who was three years old at the time, was given a sip of banana beer brewed with honey, and he got drunk and started crying. (In Rwanda it was still okay to let kids take a sip on their parents' alcoholic drink as long as they didn't drink much. The thinking was that they wouldn't like the taste of beer and then wouldn't ask to taste it until they became teenagers and started to think drinking was cool.) Xaverine's sister, who had returned from Burundi, where she had been a refugee for thirty years, had settled in Gashora, so we decided to stop there, visit her, and rest before we continued our peregrination to Kigali.

The next morning, we took a bus to Kigali. Unlike the other times when I went to Kigali before the genocide and the war, this time I did not feel as excited. Whenever I had feelings of excitement, the thought of my missing parents and siblings came to disrupt my joy. But that day was relatively better than the previous days or weeks when I was running for my life and did not know whether Lily and Valery were alive. I was grateful to have them with me and to see my cousins.

The city of Kigali was in ruins. Though most houses were still standing, they were perforated by bullets, or were missing a roof, or a side. The roads were hollowed out by bombs, and trenches stretched alongside them. We went by many cars that had been blown up by rockets. One of them was a jeep at the corner of Tapis Rouge, the dusty soccer field next to Nyamirambo soccer stadium. It had been blown up by an RPA rocket as it transported explosives for the EX-FAR (the Hutu government's national army).

As we approached my uncle's house, my cousins Petit, Bebe Muto, and Bebe Mukuru were sitting outside the fence staring at every passing car, and especially the military convoys that drew our curiosity as kids. As soon as they spotted us, they came running and screaming our names. Petit, who was my age-mate and namesake, was wearing a black shirt and black pants that matched his dark-skinned body. I was wearing green home-sewn shorts, and I felt a little embarrassed that I looked like a village boy. I would later get teased about my homemade green pants, and how village-like I looked in them, but that day there was no teasing. We hugged and they helped us carry our few bags, including one that held a bunch of plantains. My home province, the eastern province, was the bread basket of plantains and bananas, and it was tradition that every time friends from Kigali came to my town, or when we visited them, we gave them plantains.

We arrived in the house and greeted everybody. We were offered food and drinks as the tradition required, and as soon as we were done, Petit and his curious friends invited me to go play with them. I was very playful but too shy to play with my new city friends, who were far more informed about trendy, cool stuff I had never before seen. They had toys and bicycles that I did not have in my town. In my village, bicycles were vehicles, not toys for kids to play with. They were as important for the good running of a household as a truck is to a rural American farmer. Bicycles transported people to church, school, or to visit friends who lived as far as a hundred miles away. They carried loads much heavier than them. They were our buses, cabs and ambulances. They even transported the bride and groom to their religious and civil weddings.

At night, I was elated at having electricity in a house on streets that were well lit. At my village home, we did not have electricity and our big house was sometimes scary to stay in at night. That night, we sat by the front gate and played the car-counting game. We split into two teams and counted cars going in both directions. Most freeways in Kigali were two-lane roads ,so each team would count cars going in one direction and the other would count cars going in the opposite direction. Whoever counted more cars before we went back inside would win. We did not have games designed and sold to us like kids in the West. We mostly created our own games, and our own toys. My favorite toys were cars that we made from galvanized steel wire or paper boxes of juice or milk. We even made their lights using radio batteries and flashlight bulbs.

At dinner, we all sat at the table and shared stories about the war and genocide. My uncle's family had lost two of their kids. We did not know the circumstances in which Kennedy had died. As for Kayitesi, she was killed during the war with the RPA and EX-FAR when fragments from a rocket exploded in front of the house as she stood at the gate. The rest of my uncle's family had survived all odds, given that Aunt Xaverine was Tutsi and a member of Parti Libéral, which supported the RPF, and my uncle was also a member of the Parti Libéral, too. After all, they had helped raise funds to support the RPF war and had gone to the Parliament to welcome the 600 RPA soldiers, escorted by the Blue Helmets, to Kigali, to protect opposition leaders during the power-sharing process with the then government.

Xaverine told us that during the 100 days of the genocide she hid in a narrow, dark room that contained old furniture and construction materials from the time my uncle had renovated the house. For three months, she would only come out of hiding at night to eat. She stayed in hiding during the day, curled beneath pieces of old furniture. Everyone at home, even my cousins who were five years old at the time, were briefed to tell anyone who asked about their mother that she had gone to Kibungo to look for their brother Kennedy and never made it back.

The militiamen attacked and searched their house on multiple occasions but never found Xaverine. My uncle was tortured to reveal the whereabouts of his wife several times, but he never cracked. He was even shot at, but the bullet missed him by inches. When I arrived at my uncle's house, the bullet hole was still visible in the wall. He had also been taken about three times to the mass grave to be executed, but every time, someone he had once helped would show up and save his life. As the idiom goes in Kinyarwanda, God would shield him with His hand.

I came to learn that their lives were spared mainly because the chief of the militia, named Sadosi, had decided he would kill them at the end of the genocide. He had stored everything he had looted in their house with the hope that he would kill them and take their house with everything they owned and what he had pillaged.

It was dangerous to go out during the genocide but they had to buy food and fetch water somehow, so my cousin Jean de Dieu, who had the least stereotypically Tutsi looks, was the one who went grocery shopping and ran other errands for the household. As the RPA gained more territory and was defeating the EX-FAR, Sadosi, the chief of the militia in the sector was threatening to kill my uncle's family. Every day that passed they feared for their lives.

Then Fidèle, Xaverine's brother, who was also hiding with her in the same narrow space, made a bold decision. They had heard that the RPA had conquered the hill of Rebero and Kivugiza and were positioned in the Khadafi Mosque near Nyamirambo Stadium. At night, Fidèle crawled out of the house, followed the drainage ditches alongside the road, waited until daylight, and made it to the compound of the Khadafi Mosque in the territory occupied by the RPA. He told them how Sadosi was planning to kill my uncle's family and asked for their protection. They instructed the soldier who was in the minaret of the mosque to shoot anyone who approached my uncle's house. The Khadafi Mosque's spire gave them the view of the whole city, and my uncle's house was about three-quarters of a mile from the mosque. From that morning, everyone who approached my uncle's house was shot. The house-helper who tried to take a coat that hung on the rope in the front yard missed being struck by a bullet by inches, and the coat still had a hole from the bullet when we arrived at the house.

A few weeks after our arrival at my uncle's, Lily and Valery went to stay with my aunt Sidonia, who lived a few minutes from my uncle's house. After they left, I only saw them on some occasions. Especially now after they left, my new life was bittersweet. I loved the fact that I lived in the city, but I still mourned the absence of my parents and other siblings. Movies, soccer, and other outdoor games became my escape. I loved Jean-Claude Van Damme's films and imitated his fighting style—especially the kicks. Thus I earned respect from my peers. I was also one of the fastest runners among my friends. Every time we played a game that involved running, I would be picked first, which boosted my self-esteem.

July 4, 1994 marked the end of the war and we celebrated the victory of the RPF. On New Year's Eve, the whole neighborhood came to my uncle's house. We cooked beef, rice, plantain and potato fries, and drank soda, which we only did on special occasions. Adults drank beer and my uncle drank a lot of whisky—his favorite beverage.

We had guests from the Burundian, Ugandan, and Congolese diasporas but most were family friends who had survived the genocide and recently come out of hiding. It was a moment of elation and jubilation. We danced the whole night to Kayirebwa's songs and Congolese music until dawn. People had lost many loved ones. Families had been separated. But that night everyone forgot about their sorrows and the tragedies they had gone through, and celebrated together. Across the road, in the National Bank of Rwanda's residence houses, RPF cadres and soldiers shot in the air. The whole city was lit with all kinds of bullets flying in the sky, and animated with the rhythmic music of gunfire. Almost every soldier in Kigali shot some bullets in the air that night at midnight. We would later learn that those who did not have permission to shoot were punished.

Some neighbors who had grown up in Burundi were terrified by the sound of gunfire and thought that the war had resumed, so they fled to our house. I was also alarmed by the sound, but when I saw everyone cheering and screaming with joy, I joined in, even though deep inside, I was a little frightened and confused. This was the same army that had shot through our camp and had killed my grandfather and cousin, but now we were cheering them and celebrating their victory. I wondered whether it was over and which side was killing people and why. It did not make sense to me. I told myself that because I was with my uncle, they would not kill me. I did not know what it was about me that had made them want to kill me and my family.

"Was I on the wrong side of the war?" I wondered.

The celebratory atmosphere quickly faded and gave way to somber mourning of loved ones. The wounds were freshly bleeding both metaphorically and literally. Everyone I knew had lost loved ones. Everyone who was in Rwanda had lost loved ones. Even the 1959 Tutsi returnees from neighboring countries had lost loved ones who joined the RPF war. Families had been separated. Millions of Rwandans were displaced both internally and across the border in Zaïre, Burundi, and Tanzania. Hatred and mistrust loomed among those who had stayed in Rwanda. Bodies of the victims of the genocide were found on the ground, in rivers, and in deep holes. Most people did not know where their loved ones were buried or thrown.

One day we heard of a hole in the neighborhood where the bodies of my friend Cedric's parents had been thrown, so we all went to search for them among hundreds of corpses, which were by then mostly just bones wearing clothes. After being unearthed, the bodies were displayed on blue-and-white tents spread on the ground, tents provided by UNHCR (the UN Refugee Agency). Survivors would look closely and try to identify the bodies of their loved ones. There were no DNA tests, and sometimes one was not entirely sure whether who they saw was their loved ones or not. It was mostly by looking at the height of the skeleton, the clothes they wore, or any identification paper they carried in their pockets that people could identify their loved ones. The screaming of women and children was despairing. The atmosphere was mournful. Faces of mourners were distorted by a vengeful rage—and rightly so. The men who dug up bodies all looked shamefaced. I wondered whether they had been responsible for the genocide. My friends and I froze with fear and confusion. I did not know what to feel. I had never seen that many dead people.

Some deceased members of my friend Cedric's family were eventually found, and we would attend a ceremony to give them a decent burial. I feared my parents and siblings might also be dead. I had no news of them. Would I ever see them again? How would I react to the sight of their corpses? I wondered.

But the light deep inside me never extinguished. I was not physically with them but they were alive in me, in many happy memories with them that I cherished. I could still hear their voices—especially my mom's. I knew they loved me, and I still loved them. I was eight years old but somehow I knew love was undying. I still missed them.

Living Like an Orphan

The time I spent at my uncle's house would change my life forever. First, I would learn that no one can replace one's own mother or father. My uncle, being the wealthiest person in my mother's family, had always supported my cousins whose parents had died, or who had limited means to raise them, and most of them had stayed at his house. In Rwandan culture, when a child lost their parents they stayed with the closest relative, who took them in as their own child. At the end of the genocide and war, the country had a few working adults supporting many orphans. My uncle and his wife were very generous and kind to take me in with their family when my parents were not with me. But I would soon realize that however much they tried, they would not give me the same love and care I would have received from my own parents.

As kids, we were supposed to help with most of the chores, including mopping the house, doing the dishes, and running errands such as grocery shopping or taking a message to a family friend. There were no cellphones then and many people did not have landline phones, not even in the capitol city, so kids were usually the messengers. Though both my cousins and I were supposed to do an equal number of chores, sometimes they refused to do them—a luxury I did not feel entitled to. They could sit on their mother's lap and act spoiled, but I knew that was not a privilege I could afford. I always felt like an outsider whose presence at my uncle's house was a burden rather than a right of every child to have a loving family. For two years, I would experience the life of an orphan. Sometimes, I retreated to the older boys' quarters, and cried. Donat, who was the first child of my aunt Xaverine, born to her before she met my uncle, was usually the one who asked me how I was doing and consoled me. My uncle was his stepdad, and I soon realized that he must have understood my pain since he was also growing up without a father.

Then in 1996, we heard that my parents and siblings were in a refugee camp in Congo and that they were alive. However, we did not receive any letters or messages from them. Every night on the news, I would see people of all ages dying of cholera in refugee camps in Congo, and I would look carefully to see if I could identify any of them as my family members. I constantly lived with the fear that my parents and siblings would die from diseases or violence in the camps.

My uncle and his wife raised us with harsh discipline— one might even say they were abusive. Every mistake would be followed by excessive corporal punishment. In fact, my uncle was known in the neighborhood for his harsh corporal punishments. When he got angry, he punished us with all his strength. He would beat us with the closest object in his reach. When he beat us, we often ended up bruised and injured. Every morning he would come wake us up with a big stick so we could do a few chores before we went to school. All the boys stayed in an annexed house. My cousin Patrick and I were the same age, and he was the one who had the same nickname, Petit. So when I came to live with them, I was called Petit Mukuru (the older Petit), and he was called Petit Muto (the younger Petit). They only called me older because I was taller, but in actual sense Patrick was older. He had had polio as a kid, which had affected his growth. Both Patrick and I wet the bed at night but I probably did so more often than he did. Every morning my uncle would come check whether we had wet the bed, in which case we would be beaten up seriously. Though he beat us, we never stopped wetting the bed. The fear and trauma of his punishment did not seem to correct the outcome at all. Every morning I would wake up with so much fear that I might have wet the bed, and if I had, I would do everything I could to hide the impact, including mopping the room or turning the mattress over. It was shameful to take the mattress out in the sun to dry, so most of the time, we would just keep turning the mattress or put a lot of clothes on the spot we had wet, and waited until it dried.

Petit and I had felt the wrath of my uncle more than any other kid, except Depite, another cousin, who was once beaten to the point that he had a swollen face and had to wear sunglasses to school. He had stolen his mother's gold necklace and sold it on the black market. That day, my uncle beat him with every object he could reach, and neighbors had to intervene to stop him lest he kill his own son. After that day, Patrick and I resolved that every time we suspected that my uncle was going to beat us, we would run away and come back when his anger had cooled down.

My day came one afternoon when I was sent to the Nyamirambo market to buy groceries. I was very playful, and often absent-minded. I left the house and walked down to the market by the house of our Arab friends, Muselemu and Selemani. Then I passed by a house where kids were playing soccer and I told myself I would play for a few minutes and go to the market after. My shorts did not have any pockets, so I held the money and the shopping bag in my hands as I played. When I finished playing I continued my errand to the market. I was a few feet to the market when I realized that I did not have the money anymore. I quickly returned to the place where I had played with the other kids, looked around everywhere, turned every stone, but did not find the money. I walked back along the way I had taken, scrutinized every corner but did not find the money. I was terrified and started crying. I could not imagine looking in the eyes of my uncle and telling him that I had lost the money. It was the second time I had lost money. The first time, I had been lucky. The person who picked up the money had given it back to me, after walking with me to my house to get confirmation from my uncle's wife that it was indeed the amount she had given me. I had been sent to buy bread scraps at Karinda Sweet Bread's Bakery to make meatballs.

I walked home dragging my feet. My uncle's wife Xaverine owned a convenience store in one of the annexed houses. She was there when I arrived home, and to my biggest misfortune, my uncle was also there with his friends drinking whisky. I entered the shop, almost tiptoeing, petrified and embarrassed, with guilt and fear unconcealed on my face. I approached my uncle's wife, who stood behind the counter, and told her that I had lost the money. I was trying to speak as low as I could, but she exclaimed, "You lost the money, again!"

Then my uncle who was sitting in the corner of the store sipping his whisky overheard us. He stood as quickly as he could, turned to me and reached for his bottle of whisky to hit me with it. My instinct told me to run but he was closer to the door than I was. I dived through the only window that was open, and my right shin hit on the lower part of the window frame. I almost broke my tibia. I picked myself up as quickly as I could and ran through the gate.

As I passed the gate, I almost bumped into my uncle, who had run around to come and catch me, but I was lighter and faster, even after injuring my leg. He was obese, and must have been drunk, so I had an advantage over him. When I knew I was far enough that he would not catch me, I stopped and cried. He ordered me to walk to him and face my sentence but I refused. I knew him enough to understand that he would injure me if he beat me in his drunken state. I ran away and swore not to go back home that night. Butera, our former house-helper, worked at a charcoal business in the neighborhood, which he also guarded at night. I asked him whether he could let me stay with him at night, and to my greatest relief he agreed. I had contemplated staying with some of the family friends, but I was afraid that my uncle would send someone to fetch me. I was also terrified at the idea of spending the night on the street in the open.

Butera's store was a tent that sheltered hundreds of charcoal bags that he supplied to the whole neighborhood. He had no bed or mattress, so at night we slept on empty charcoal bags that surprisingly kept us warm despite the discomfort of charcoal dust. But I did not have the luxury to choose where I would spend the night. Comfort was not my priority, security was. I slept like a baby that night, without any fear that anyone would break into the tent and do us harm. The tent felt more secure than my uncle's house that night even though it did not have the same comfort. I learned that security and safety were the most important needs. I did not have dinner that night but I felt safe.

Looking back, I understand why some kids leave their homes where they don't feel loved and protected and choose to live on the streets. My uncle was not a bad person, but that night he was drunk and angry, and he had anger management issues. We had learned how to manage him. When he was not drunk or angry, he was a nice person who told us many old stories, including the one about how he came to the city from the village and managed to become a driver at the Belgian embassy at eighteen years of age. He would tell us how he was stopped by extremist Bakiga military and questioned about how he had gotten the job, saying, "Tutsis are so sly! How did you get a job at the Belgian embassy?" At that time moving from any district to the capital city required a laissez-passer (a local passport). That is how stifling and constraining the policies of the first republic of the 1960s were.

My uncle had prevailed all odds and the only way for him to get a good job without connections was to work for White people. At that time, being a driver of White people was a decent job, and it still is today. As I grew up, I also understood that he had had a rough childhood. His father had left them with my grandmother, married another wife and established his home in Gatare. Through my aunt, I would also learn that my maternal grandfather was Hutu, from Gatare, and had been an indentured servant of a Tutsi chief named Gasore, from Burasa, so he could get cattle and land. His master would eventually give him cows and land in exchange for marrying his daughter, a spinster who needed a husband. My grandfather would marry her and leave my grandmother, his first wife. The house and land where my mother grew up were part of the property my grandfather had been given by his master. This is the social mobility price he had to pay to become "Tutsi." This is why my mother would grow up without a father, and why my uncle dropped out of school so he could work and take care of his sisters. My step-grandmother would have twins, Hitimana and Abimana (whose daughter Mapua was with me when my grandfather was killed), and another son, Generali. My aunt spoke very highly of her stepmother's kindheartedness. After her children grew up and left the house, my grandfather's second wife, Madeleine, decided to leave my grandfather. He had a reputation of being tight-fisted. He would not even spend money to buy basic household items like soap or salt—very likely because of growing up in so much scarcity.

My mother and her sisters had continued their schooling, but my uncle dropped out of high school and went to Kigali to hustle to pay his sisters' tuition. He had not forgiven his father. He always reminded his children how spoiled they were. He told us stories of the natives of Kigali from whom he bought his land, reminding us how unlikely it was that one could make it in the city if they were born there because they took the opportunities for granted.

My friends and I found ways to escape the harsh reality of genocide, war, and the ongoing uncertainty. In fact, war became our game. My peers and I woke up early and went jogging with soldiers from Tapis-Rouge to Camp Kigali. I enjoyed the rhythmic songs they intoned as we ran. Mucakamucaka was the name of the military rhythmic jogging that was accompanied with songs—some of them with sexually inappropriate content for kids. We played war games by carrying toy guns made from metal scraps, or anything we could make toy guns out of. Edem, who was older than the rest of us, was our commander in chief, mostly because he resembled Paul Kagame, the leader of the Rwanda Patriotic Army, or PC, as we called him. Kids spread all kinds of rumors. One of them was that there was going to be another war, and only those with an RPF tattoo would survive.

As kids, we naively believed the rumors and scarred our thighs and arms with RPF tattoos. Our world was that of war and our heroes were the victors of the war.

The wounds of the genocide and war were still fresh, and the country was desperately trying to rebuild before it healed. At school, landmines left behind by the defeated army blew up children every day. Bodies of those who had died in the genocide were routinely exhumed to be buried in decency. The first perpetrators of the genocide were being brought to justice. The excitement of a victorious end of the war slowly faded into a sudden realization of the enormity of pain, loss, and devastation of the genocide and war. I was there. In the middle of it. At eight to ten years old. I was lonely and traumatized. I was quite an intelligent kid, but my performance at school suffered to the point where I had to repeat Primary Four. I needed to make sense of the whole mess, but my young head could not wrap itself around the complexity of the Rwandan apocalypse. I was a child. I needed family. Love. Security.

The Military Tribunal was about one mile from my uncle's house, to the left of the Tapis Rouge intersection that we crossed to Kivugiza Primary School. The only memories of the early trials included Frodouard Karamira's trial. From what I heard, he had been born in a Tutsi family but later chose to become Hutu. He was accused of co-creating the bloodthirsty Interahamwe militia, and of personally killing hundreds of fellow Tutsis, including members of his own family. This only added confusion to my understanding of the conflict and the already convoluted nature of ethnic identification in Rwanda. The news of his arrest and trial was all over the news, and I remember seeing dozens of reporters waiting outside the tribunal as he was being tried.

I would also witness the first execution of the genocide

convicts by a firing squad at Tapis Rouge wearing ninja hoodies. While all of this was going on, the adults did not comfort us or at least reassure us that everything would be okay. Instead, they mostly projected their anger to us when we slightly misbehaved. Rwanda was a traumatized nation. My friends and I were terrified.

The Big Reunion

In 1996, after Rwanda invaded Congo, helped Kabila take power from Mobutu, and destroyed the refugee camps, waves of refugees returned to the country. The news was filled with images of hungry, exhausted refugees crossing the border. I was excited that my family could be part of the returning tides of refugees, but I had no assurance that they would be, since we did not have any way of communicating with them.

Then one day, my uncle brought the news to us. My father, my sister Kiki, and my brother Thierry had made it back to Rwanda and were in my village in Eastern Rwanda. Later that week, Lily, Valery, and I would take a bus to our home in Zaza to be reunited with them. I was almost in disbelief and so excited that I did not know how to react to the news. We heard that my father had returned without my mother, so that halved my joy; but I was still elated at the thought of seeing him and my two siblings who had returned with him.

We took a bus from Nyamirambo, where my uncle lived,

to Nyabugogo, the main bus station where buses to different provinces park, and then another bus to Zaza. The road conditions were substandard and the driver had to maneuver around multiple potholes in the road. I was impatient to see my family, so the time it took to get to my village seemed to have tripled.

News of our arrival had reached home before us. The bus dropped us on the main road at about noon, and we took the narrow path that cut through thick banana plantations to our house. We greeted people along the way who recognized us and remarked how much we had grown in two years. When we arrived at the home of my paternal uncle Rudoviko, who lived a few feet from our house, we passed my brother Thierry standing in their front yard, at first not recognizing him. He had grown, but he also wore dirty clothes and had dust all over his body and his face. We had been living in the city for two years, so we looked cleaner than the average village kid.

My uncle Rudoviko's family was living next to their house in a tent provided by UNHCR (the UN Refugee Agency) because their home was occupied by a family of 1959 refugees who had returned from Burundi. Refugees who were part of the earlier Rwandan diasporas in neighboring countries had returned after the victory of the RPF. The family in my uncle's house had left Rwanda thirty years before, so they did not own any property. Most of the 1959 revolution refugees' properties had been distributed by the government or taken over by their neighbors, who had sold them to other people. When they returned after the 1994 genocide and war, most of them did not return to the places where their parents or grandparents had lived before they were forced into exile. Some of them did not even know where their parents had lived thirty years before, so they occupied houses and land left behind by Hutus who had fled the advance of RPF.

We stopped at my uncle's tent and greeted him and his family before we continued to our house. My father and sister Kiki were standing in front of our house as we approached. We went down to the other side of our field, where my mother had grown corn, and where the two avocado trees I liked to climb still stood. We went around the trees, and as soon as my father recognized us, he walked quickly towards us, lifted Valery in the air and hugged him. He did the same to Lily and me. He is quite a hugger. I felt his love through the strain of his hug and realized how much I had missed his embrace.

We also greeted my sister Kiki, and as soon as we were done, Thierry came forward, and our father reintroduced us to him. He was shy and did not seem to understand what was going on, nor even to know he had other siblings. In fact, I doubt that anyone had prepared him for our arrival. He was just one year old when they fled to Congo, so he did not remember any of us.

It did not take me long to realize how much my father had changed. He had lost a lot of weight and was aged from the ordeal of the exodus, living as a refugee, enduring the separation from his children, and losing his sweetheart.

We headed to my paternal grandmother's house, which was about fifty feet from our house. She gave us the longest hug and uttered manifold blessings. My uncle Thomas' wife, Vianney, had also returned from Tanzania with her two children and my cousin Mutima, who had stayed behind with her nanny. Vianney was staying with my grandmother, since my uncle had not returned with her and she was afraid of living alone with her children in their house, which was isolated from other houses on the outskirts of the parish forest. My grandmother lived alone, so she was happy to stay with her daughter-in-law.

My father, who also wanted to stay near my grandmother, spent his days at her house. They all cooked together and shared everything. My father and siblings only went to our house to sleep. Now my grandmother's house was where we all had our meals and received guests. Meanwhile, we shared our house with two young families that each had a child. The couples had married in refugee camps and did not have homes in Rwanda, so my father offered them a room each. We had a six-bedroom house so there was no shortage of space, and in fact we liked sharing it with other people because otherwise it would have felt too big for us.

Lily and Valery stayed with the rest of the family, but I would go back to Kigali to finish the academic year before I could return to stay with my family permanently. I was happy to have reunited with one of my parents and the rest of my siblings, but deep inside I missed my mother.

I learned that she and my father had been separated during a Rwandan Army raid on refugees in the Democratic Republic of Congo when ADFL (Alliance of Democratic Forces for the Liberation of Congo) and the Rwanda Defense Force overthrew President Mobutu's regime in what has been called the First Congo War. Just as they had shot through the internally displaced people at Kanazi when I was separated from my family, the soldiers attacked crowds of refugees in Congo by surprise and killed thousands of people. As they fled, my mother ended up running in a different direction from my father and two siblings. My father faced the choice of leaving my two siblings during the gunfire to go find my mother, or stick with his children and run for safety while hoping that my mother would somehow survive and reunite with them. He ultimately felt he only had one choice and he ran with my siblings as far from gunfire as he could. They ran away into the Congolese rainforest, through tall, fat trees that some said could swallow people whole. They jumped over dead bodies and passed by babies whose parents had been shot, some of them still suckling their dead mothers' breasts.

They wandered in the forest for months, hoping to reach a road or a village where people lived and ask for directions, but the forest was just too vast. They walked until their shoes fell apart and until the sweat dried on their brows. My father's feet have never recovered from the exodus. He carried my brother Thierry on his back and held my sister Kiki's hand. One night, they said, they slept at the foot of a huge tree only to awaken and find a deep hole that they could have easily fallen into without knowing. They fed on wild taro roots that my father still believes were manna from heaven. They crossed rivers, sometimes by cutting a tall tree on one side of the riverbank, letting it fall across, and then using it to traverse the waters. The rivers were very deep and the trees could only support a few people. Families would take turns crossing the river, balancing on the tree, and sometimes people would panic and fall into the river and drown. Every time a family member crossed, the rest of the family on either side of the river would pray that they would make it to safety.

Rebuilding

I went back to Kigali determined to do better in school. For the first time in three years, I felt I had a reason to do well: I had someone who would be proud of me if I succeeded, and that was enough of an incentive for me to improve my academic performance. My father had asked me to at least get seventy percent in the last trimester. To everyone's surprise, I ended the term with a score of exactly seventy percent.

In the summer of 1997, I returned to Zaza to stay with my family. The transition from the city back to my village was bittersweet at first. I missed having electricity and playing with my friends, and especially watching Hollywood action movies. My best friend Blaise had been killed in the genocide, and there were not many kids of my age who understood me in my village. It would not take me long to realize that life would never be like before, but the village was not short of adventures I could embark on. After a few weeks, I had adjusted to my new home, my real home.

101

My father did not have his teaching job at first, so he had to do some construction odd-jobs to provide for us. He did not wear the suits or well-ironed shirts and slacks he wore before the genocide and war. We were not the sons and daughters of a schoolteacher that we once were. But by far, the most obvious change was the absence of my mother at the dinner table and on Sundays when we all went to mass. Her physical absence left such a vacuum in our lives, but her spiritual presence was always there. I still heard her voice whenever I was afraid, telling me to be bold; or when I got discouraged, telling me that everything would be okay. Sometimes I would see women who looked like her on the streets, and I'd follow them, only to realize that they were not my mother. I developed strong connections with many mothers, as if she had pleaded with every mother I came across to look after me on her behalf, and indeed they would take care of me without even knowing my story.

When fall came, my father asked me whether I wanted to repeat Primary Four, since I had not done very well overall. In his absence, I had not taken school seriously; all that mattered to me was playing and watching movies—anything that helped me escape my perceived reality of being an orphan. But I insisted that I would go to Primary 5 and study hard to catch up on what I had missed. My father agreed to let me go to Primary Five on the condition that I would be among the top ten of my class.

I had to catch up on a lot of things. I soon realized that I did not even know all the multiples of three by heart, so I had to memorize the whole multiplication table, which I should have done three years earlier in Primary Two. I had not been motivated to study after the genocide, and the teachers themselves were traumatized. Looking back, I am certain that my one-armed Primary Three teacher, Kaboko, had post-traumatic stress disorder (PTSD). He was a war veteran and had lost his arm during the RPF armed struggle. His punishments were the harshest. He would tell us to remove our shoes and then beat us on the soles of our feet until we were too sore to walk.

This teacher's actions were not the only peril we students faced—there was plenty of peer-to-peer bullying, as well. My friends who had brothers or relatives who were in the military would bring them in on the last day of school to punish whoever had bullied them. I was very athletic and had a muscular "six-pack" at age ten, but I did not have anyone in my family who was in the military, so I was nice to kids, and I played at karate to make myself appear tough. (I loved martial arts, especially Jean-Claude Van Damme's fighting style, as mentioned earlier.)

When the end of the academic year came, to everyone's surprise, I was among the top five of my class. It should not have been a surprise, since prior to the genocide, I was always top of my class. I knew I was smart. I just wasn't motivated before my father returned from exile. Doing better in school increased my confidence, and I discovered I had sharp curiosity and a deep love for learning the causes of things.

The following year, my last year of primary school, I would do even better and be the best performer in the whole district. I had passed both the national and the seminary exams. My father asked me to choose where I wanted to study. The seminary was an all-boys Catholic school, and seminaries were some of the most competitive schools in Rwanda. The only problem was that they were partly private, and hence more expensive for my father. He had regained his teaching job, but the salary was meager and irregular, and the government owed teachers many salary arrears. My sister Lily was also in a boarding school far from our hometown, and my younger sister Kiki would go to secondary school the following year, straining my father's humble income. He knew the seminary was my first choice, so he let me choose it. He also wanted me to go there since it was the only way to get the best education in the whole country cheaply.

To add to the hurdles, a policy was enforced that would change our lives. The government, through Imidugudu Policy, forced everyone who lived far from the main road to destroy their houses and move into the plots assigned for settlements. The reason they gave was that it would be easy to bring infrastructure to people if they lived closer to each other than if they were scattered around the hills. But some people said that it was a move by the government to make it easy to control people in a period when there was still mistrust and fear of insurgency. People were supposed to obey without asking questions, and they well knew that the consequences for disobedience would be severe. We were given a few corrugated iron sheets, and left alone to build new houses in Imidugudu (settlements). The only group that would receive help building their houses was that of the survivors of the genocide against the Tutsi.

Our six-room house stood on a hill, surrounded by banana plantations and kraals for cows and goats, and chicken and rabbit coops. We grew everything we ate, from plantains to beans, sweet potatoes, potatoes, peanuts, and peas. We lived close to our fields, which made it easy for us to look after them. This was the house where my two parents got married and where my siblings and I were born and grew up. It was where we celebrated Christmas and baptisms for all my siblings and myself. It was where I learned to crawl and walk, where my father played the guitar to us as we waited for dinner, and where I learned to climb avocado and mango trees. My father had saved for many years from the time he started teaching, at age seventeen, to build it and completed its construction when he was in his late twenties. He had hoped he would retire there.

This was not to be. A meeting was called and people were told that if they did not comply with the order, the authorities would come and destroy their houses. Rumors started circulating that the government wanted to group everyone together so they could kill them more easily. Despite the rumors, everyone without exception complied. We helped our father dismantle our house brick after brick. Everyone destroyed their own homes and went about building new, but much worse, houses on the plots they were assigned.

People were so fearful, resentful, distrustful, and guilt-ridden, but as kids, we were excited about moving to the main road, where we would see cars and lights. The idea of living in an urban environment was, and still is, romanticized in Rwanda, making people who live in the countryside feel ashamed of their roots, while those living in the city snobbishly look down upon their rural countrymen. While we jubilated about our move, my father was mourning the whole time he demolished his own house. At times a brick would fall and miss him by inches. We helped carry the corrugated tin sheets to our new house and the wood that we would use as firewood for many years that followed.

Though it was a sad time for him, we were lucky to own another house on the main road. It had been a bakery and a convenience store, so we moved there. I helped him remodel it and add two rooms to it. But whatever he did to our new home, it would look nothing like our old house. And, although I enjoyed living in our new humble home, it would never truly feel like my home. Even today when I dream about home, I see the images of our old six-room house. I see the kraals of our cattle in the back-yard and the avocado trees in front of our gate. I see the many mango trees we climbed every December, both around our house and on our way to and from school. I see the very corner where my father built the nativity set at Christmastime and where my mother sat as she prepared mandazi (donuts).

Most people destroyed their big comfortable houses and built houses that were not even paved or had proper floors, drastically changing their socio-economic status. Many widows did not find a place to stay until later, when people were done building their houses and helped them. My uncle Thomas' wife Vianney stayed with us with her three children until my father helped her repair her house. My grandmother would also stay with us. The house was crowded, but as kids we did not seem to mind. We were excited about having a lot of civilization around us, especially the children from Burundi who told us stories about what life was like in that country, and whom I would befriend by leveraging my athletic and acrobatic skills that I had acquired in Kigali.

The Rwandan social fabric was made up of sub-groups because of a tragic history that separated families, neighbors, and citizens. Under the two major divisions of Hutus and Tutsis, there were also diasporas. Families that had fled the 1959 massacres of Tutsis and the persecutions that followed, had grown up in neighboring countries, and some in farther lands, where they adopted different cultures and spoke different languages. The four major groups were: Abarundi, or those who grew up in Burundi; Abaganda or Abasajya, those who grew up in Uganda; and Abasopecya or Abanyarwanda, those who stayed in Rwanda and were both Hutus and survivors of the genocide against the Tutsi. There were also those who grew up in Congo, Tanzania, Kenya, and several other countries.

Language was also another divider. Burundi, Congo, and Rwanda were francophone countries, which made diasporas from those countries francophone, but Uganda was an Anglophone country, and most of the new military and political leaders had grown up in Uganda and hence spoke English. President Kagame himself could not deliver a speech in Kinyarwanda without mixing in some English words—at times he used more English than Kinyarwanda. The conjunction, "so" became very common to use, as did the word, "sorry." Even today, those who do not speak English will say "sorry," to apologize for a mistake or will use "so" in whatever ways they please, sometimes in syntactically incorrect places.

Most people socialized more with people who shared the same provenance, dating back three decades, but I did not seem to care. Instead, I took intense pleasure in breaking the dividing walls and relished the cultural diversity within the Rwandan citizenry. My new best friend was named Picu, and I spent most of my time with him. He was a talented soccer player and an incredible dribbler. He and his family were our neighbors, and we did everything together, from playing soccer, to fetching water, and grazing goats. I did not see Picu as Umurundi (the singular form of Abarundi, used to describe those Rwandan returnees from Burundi). He did not see me as Umusopecya (the singular form of Abasopecya, a name given to Rwandans—both Tutsi genocide survivors and Hutus—who never left the country). Our friendship brought our two families together, a testament that Rwandans from different diasporas could forge a new identity of being Rwandans and get along.

Teen Years in the Seminary

One sunny afternoon in 1999, I packed my bag and strapped it with my mattress onto the carrier of my father's bicycle. It was my first day of secondary school. Zaza Minor Seminary was just about two miles away from my house. My father followed me on his other bicycle. When we arrived, parents and their nervous sons were coming in and out of the front gate of the seminary. After paying for tuition at the bursar's office, my father escorted me to my dormitory. We had passed children who were being hazed, so I was terrified. We found a bed that was not yet occupied, and I claimed it. My father bid me farewell and left. I was on my own in this new dungeon full of hungry, testosterone-filled lions.

The first night was a nightmare. The seminary still had a tradition of hazing newcomers. Older students humiliated newcomers with semi-official permission from the authorities. Some mean students would even beat the newcomers, and whoever resisted initiation faced even harsher treatment. Some initiation practices were funny, but there were not clear limits as to what older students could make us do. Some of them would just ask you to hold the edge of their shirt and walk around the campus as if you were their slave. Others would make you guard an insect and make sure not to lose it, or force you to make a fake phone call with their smelly running shoe.

But other practices were meaner, like when a group of Senior Five students stopped my friends and me and told us to jump as they waggled a stick beneath our feet, like a jumping rope. We kept jumping, and when we stopped, the stick spun like a helicopter blade and hit us. One of my friends was heavier and less athletic than the rest of us, so he got tired and was beaten many times until he cried. After the humiliation, he had bruises on his calves. To our surprise, when he reported the incident to the animateurs, or student inspectors, they did not punish Pacifique, the older boy who had hurt my friend. Many first-year students were afraid of reporting these types of incidents to the authorities lest the older students do something even meaner and without leaving evidence of responsibility.

Some of the punishments for students who rebelled against hazing was to pour water onto their beds when they were asleep to humiliate them by making it seem that they had wetted their beds. Some older students would make newcomers do their laundry for the whole semester, on top of doing the dishes for everybody, as was the school tradition. The school system was as hierarchical as the military, in fact many people argued that it was partly modeled after military schools. First-year students were supposed to obey second year's, and so on.

In every way, first-year students were at the bottom of the chain of command, and everybody could bully them without any consequence. I abhorred the system so much so that I did not haze anyone for the six years I spent in the seminary. In fact, I was criticized for talking to younger students. I was upset that no one seemed to recognize the injustice of the whole culture, and I was determined to unapologetically undermine the oppressive norms that penalized the less powerful. It was in the seminary that I learned about my "allergy" to injustice and the extent of my stubbornness—which I believe was passed on to me from my mother. I took a lot of pleasure in breaking all the rules that did not make sense to me, including skipping mass—one of the gravest offenses you could commit in a Catholic school.

Ultimately, my seminary experience was positive overall. In the seminary, I would learn to study independently, be punctual, and most importantly, I would discover and harness my love for books and knowledge. Every week we had to read a book and present it in front of the class. The seminary's three guiding principles were science, santé, et sainté (science, good health, and holiness). We had to excel in academics, sports, and good character. Three phrases summarized what one needed to do to avoid trouble: Do the right thing, in the right place, at the right time. This meant that we were all supposed to do the same thing at the same time. If everyone else was playing and you were studying, then you were doing the wrong thing, at the wrong time, in the wrong place.

Everybody had the same amount of time to study, and it was forbidden to study while others participated in a different activity. Waking up at night to catch up with school work while others slept was out of question, even if you had been sick. We had some of the strictest teachers, and a grammatical or spelling error on a geography or math test, including forgetting a stress in a word, cost you points. At the end of year, there were always kids we knew would get expelled from school because their grades weren't good enough or because of disciplinary reasons. The third trimester was the toughest for them. When they realized that they could not make up for the grades they had lost in the previous trimesters, they became disillusioned, depressed, or kwiranda, as we called it, and some of them became aggressive. Most of those who were expelled from the seminary did better than most of the students in less competitive public schools.

We were supposed to speak French or English always or we would be handed a wooden padlock, or cadenat, which we would take to the animateurs (conduct supervisors) at night and get our conduct points taken away. When one had ten points subtracted from their conduct points, they were suspended for a week and had to bring their parents to school. A week away meant missing thirty classes, plus exams, quizzes, and assignments that were worth a lot of credits and that one would not be able to regain.

But overall, the seminary gave me a foundation of knowledge, discipline, and values of excellence that I hope will last forever. Some of the priests would have an everlasting influence on me, especially Father Kayisabe Vedaste, who was our academic manager and rector for nearly four years before he went to Rome to pursue his doctorate in philosophy. He was the teacher who most helped me discover my own passion for philosophy and critical thinking, which made me the free thinker I am today. Like many of my friends, I started the seminary at age thirteen, thinking I would become a priest, and I prayed about this path every day. But, after three years, I realized that the priesthood was not my vocation. When I was in Senior Five (junior high), we studied the history of the Catholic church, and that was enough to dissuade me from my initial wish to become part of the church as an institution. Though I understood that the church had changed since the Crusades and the death of Galileo,

I had learned that independent thinking was as vital to me as eating or breathing. I was too stubborn to fit into the hierarchical apparatus of the church.

I was also going through a serious crisis of faith that made me uncertain about the very existence of God and what His/Her/Its role was in our lives. I was frustrated with God, and I felt justified in that feeling. Like many Rwandans, I could not accept the fact that God had left so many innocents to be slaughtered by their fellow countrymen and had not intervened with His/Her/Its mighty powers. My argument was that, if God loved His/Her/Its children, God would have come to their rescue. If God was All-Powerful, All-Knowing, All-Merciful, and All-Loving, God would have protected children and the elderly who died in the genocide and war. If God loved me and my family, He or She would have brought back my mother and my little sister Petite, who was born in the camps, and whom I never met. Why did God let me witness the death of my grandfather? Why did God not save my cousin Mapua, who was just three years old?

I did not get any satisfying answers from the psalms we read every morning and night, nor in the sermons from the mass I had to attend every single morning without exception. I was angry with God for overlooking all the injustices and atrocities I had witnessed as a child. In fact, I argued that if God existed, God was unjust and did not love His/Her/Its creation, or was a passive God who did not intervene in our lives. My frustration led me to bring up my doubts multiple times with my friends, which earned me the labels of atheist and heretic. But I was not an atheist; deep inside me, I felt a strong connection to the Higher Being, whatever you call It.

As I tried to make sense of what my country had been through, I could not stop thinking about religion. I had learned that Jesus

Christ had abolished all ethnic barriers and unified Christians under a new kinship that was stronger than blood relations. But somehow people carrying saints' names—saints who had been martyred for standing up for their faith in God, Jesus, and the religion of love, truth, and forgiveness—had murdered their neighbors, family members, and fellow countrymen carrying those same saints' names, and right around Eastertime. The killers could see these holy names right in front of them on the identity cards they forced their victims to produce, but that did not make them think twice before they killed them. The Christian label was not important to them as long as the Tutsi label was mentioned on the identity cards. How could this be? Rwanda was and still is an overwhelmingly Christian nation. All these people went to church on Sunday looking their best, sang the same creed, and shared communion. How could that be?

Since I felt the presence of the Higher Being, it occurred to me that the problem might be in our limited, human understanding of God's nature and role in our lives, not whether He/She/It existed or not. My frustration in a way, was aimed at provoking this All-powerful Being to reveal Himself or Herself to me and teach me the Truth about His/Her/Its true essence, and the world people claimed He/She/It had created. I was frustrated by religion and by the adults around me who did not have answers to questions I thought should be important for everyone to consider. I was angry at a society that seemed to be once again making the same mistakes that had led it into an abyss of death and self-destruction. I was mad at young people who did not seem to care about these questions that I was certain affected their lives and would shape those of their offspring.

Before I realized it, I was embarking on long journey to find the Truth, or at least the glimpses of the Truth. Since neither my religion nor my culture seemed to provide me with answers, rebellion against religion and culture were my only weapons on this long and lonely journey. I would question everything I had learned, and start the long journey to relearn the Truth of God, humanity, and my very existence. My questions were not limited to spiritual matters. Post-genocide Rwanda was too divided for my taste, and since I did not neatly fit into the different "tribes" or "diasporas," it would be a lonely path I followed. I broke many societal barriers, some successfully, and others unsuccessfully. At some point, I even argued for radical solutions to prevent future divisions among Rwandans, like bringing a totally different people into the country to interbreed with Rwandans and dissolve the castes that seemed to have been hardened by the genocide and war.

Everyone seemed to be taking sides and claiming identity in a particular caste, except me. I found it hard to tell whether people were genuine with me, or whether they were hypocritical. I always asked myself whether people associated with me because of what they assumed I identified with, or whether they just liked me. I loved my country, but I began to feel that I did not want to be Rwandan, nor to have my future children to inherit the divisions that I still witnessed every day. Even though I was young and did not intend to marry anytime soon, I planned to marry outside my citizenship, and to strip myself of the Rwandan nationality as soon as I could. Rwanda did not feel like my ecological niche, at all. I felt like a fish in a river that was drying up, suffocating to death as its gills collapsed without enough surface for diffusion to take place. I was resolved to take on a new national identity, but I just did not know which, how, or when I would do so.

Talking about ethnicity was taboo. Identity cards did not

mention one's "ethnicity" after the genocide. The new government decided to remove mention of ethnic identification in official documents. Even before this point, my father had never mentioned our family's ethnicity, and I did not know how to broach the subject. But I was growing up in a country where most adults had failed in many ways to find the wisdom and courage to avoid a tragedy from befalling the country, and were afraid of sharing what they witnessed or experienced lest they mention anything that could raise controversy. Children had been the most severely affected by the conflict and were not getting the explanations from the adults who had seen the conflicts breed, escalate, and culminate into a genocide. This caused a lot of vexation and led me to rebel against adults; cultural, religious, and political institutions; and to look for answers myself. I felt lost in a hinterland of unanswered but crucial questions. I did not trust the version of the genocide narrative told by Hutus, neither did I trust that of the RPF-led government since I had survived crimes committed by RPA soldiers. Furthermore, I knew I could not talk about those crimes without causing controversy and possibly facing the wrath of powerful people who did not want anyone to tarnish their image nor to have anyone question their legitimacy—not even a child with questions about why his grandfather was murdered in front of his eyes.

Father Kayisabe

In my first year in the seminary, I did the dishes like everyone else in my class: after breakfast, lunch, and dinner. It was the school policy, and no one seemed to mind it as long as they did not have to do the dishes for the remainder of their time in the seminary. It did not bother me for the most part, except after lunch.

Sports time was after lunch, so I tried to do the dishes as fast as I could and run to the basketball court before the big kids came to play. My school only had one serviceable basketball court with multiple potholes, the other was completely unusable. My primary school did not have a basketball court, and I had played soccer barefoot like most Rwandan boys on the dusty streets and playgrounds; but I wanted to try out for basketball at the seminary since basketball players were widely regarded as the coolest kids at school.

One day, I finished doing the dishes quickly and headed to the basketball court. About ten minutes into playing with my classmates, an older boy by the name of Mirukiro came.

"I want every first-year student to have disappeared from this court by the time I reopen my eyes," he said.

Mirukiro had big, red eyes from a lack of sleep. He had a reputation of waking up in the middle of the night to study while others slept, and had earned the nickname of "the night owl." Though it was prohibited to study while others slept, Mirukiro had devised ingenious plans to escape the austere animateurs who patrolled the campus hunting down "night owls." Mirukiro's sleepless nights (nuits blanches, or dina, as we called them) paid off in subjects that required memorization like history and geography, but he did not do as well in subjects that required critical thinking. His classmates bullied him and adapted a popular radio advertisement jingle to tease him about studying at night while others slept. It went as follows:

> Igishwi muri dina, gituramye kizi guhonda.
> (The night owl that studies at night, is good at cramming.)
> Imibu ntigikanga, gifite amababa menshi.
> (He is not afraid of mosquitoes, he has lots of feathers.)

Despite being the target of such teasing (or maybe because of it), he was also one of the most feared bullies for the first-year students, so when he ordered us to leave the court, we all ran away. First I went to play volleyball at a horizontal bar for a while. Then I went to watch the volleyball team play at the old basketball court that had been transformed for that game. I was playing on the side of the court with my friend Alain when Father Kayisabe, who was the academic manager at the time, asked us whether we wanted to join the volleyball team. He was the volleyball coach, and was highly respected by all the students and staff. We both said yes, and joined the volleyball team for the ordinary level (secondary one to three). Father Kayisabe had an incredible eye for talent, and he was a great coach, mentor, and visionary. For about two years, I was the youngest player on the team. I would later become its captain after all the older players graduated. My name became synonymous with volleyball. But my athletic talents would not be the only gems Father Kayisabe would help cultivate.

When I was in Secondary Three, I started reading in mass. I was a good reader, but biblical Kinyarwanda was old and diffi-cult. Being a tonal language whose orthography has no stresses or indication of long and short vowels, Kinyarwanda was very easy to misread. In fact, I was more comfortable reading French, which had stresses or accents. In many cases, you can't guess the pronunciation of a Kinyarwanda word unless you know it. My school was very elitist and non-forgiving. Mistakes were not tolerated and perfectionism was glorified. School authorities and students alike expected excellence, and bullying was very common.

My nightmare came one Sunday when I was assigned a reading in a Kinyarwanda mass. I was horrified to speak in front of people. Mass was still very ceremonial and formal in Rwanda. We marched with priests from the sacristy to the altar, dressed in white robes. We prostrated in front of the altar, then went to our seats. After the main priest had introduced the mass, I went to give the first reading. I approached the pulpit and opened the bible, my hands visibly shaking with fear, and my eyes tearing, making the letters blurry and illegible. The whole congregation was silent, anticipating the reading. The first reading was always from the Old Testament, my least favorite books of the Bible. I had skimmed through the reading before mass but had forgotten to ask the right pronunciation of the word that would cause my embarrassment for an entire week. The reading was from Judges 6:11-23. No sooner had I commenced the first sentence than I set my eyes on the word "umushishi" (oak) and read it how I thought it read without knowing that the /i/ sound in the third syllable was long. The priest who was presiding over the mass corrected me. Though my pronunciation of the word did not mean anything funny, the congregation of students burst in laughter. I continued the reading, more horrified and embarrassed than ever. When I was done reading, I sat in the corner of the altar where all the readers sat, in front of the whole congregation. For two hours, I endured the disparaging eyes of the bullies. After mass, I left after everyone had emptied the chapel to avoid the bullies. But some bullies, especially one named Cyril, parroted the same word I had mispronounced every single time our paths crossed for the whole week.

After realizing the embarrassment I endured, Father Kayisabe gave me a chance to start over. He assigned me readings for the remainder of the week. By the end of the week I had dealt with most of my stage fright. The following year, I enrolled in the French drama club and co-founded the contemporary dance club. By the time I left high school, I was a good public speaker and an athlete, thanks to Father Kayisabe.

Father Kayisabe had survived the genocide by hiding among dead bodies in his hometown parish, after being wounded by a grenade fragment that struck him during a raid by Interahamwe militiamen. Half of his family was exterminated. He was inspired to become a priest by a Hutu priest who was killed with his Tutsi parishioners after refusing to leave them to die at the hands of Hutu radicals. Father Kayisabe had seen the worst of humanity and had decided to be the best humanity could offer. Until today, I know no other person who has so fully learned the right lessons from the genocide. I am forever grateful that he survived and was part of my life when I needed a mentor. He was a living role model for those of us who were privileged to know him. His shrewdness and meek spirit were unmatched by anyone I knew. When he left to do his doctorate, the whole congregation burst in tears during a farewell mass. He was the embodiment of love, wisdom, acute intelligence, and kindness. He and my father remain my two most consequential male role models.

Go Ask Your Ethnicity

After graduating from seminary, I went to university at the Kigali Institute of Education (now called the University of Rwanda, College of Education). Those years were a time of stability, or even stasis, for me, and I don't find much to document. After leaving the university, I began to push myself in new ways to confront what I had survived as a child.

In 2012 I went to meet with the director of the Kigali Genocide Memorial, Freddy, and his deputy, Solange. I had passed the job interview for the position of the public relations manager at the memorial and was going to discuss the salary. When I left the memorial, it was around noon. My girlfriend, Jeannette, was in the Nyabugogo bus station with a relative who was supposed to take a bus to Kampala. We had agreed earlier that day to have lunch after my meeting at the memorial, so as soon as my meeting concluded, I joined her at the bus station and we ate at a restaurant on the second floor of one of the buildings overlooking the bus station.

Jeanette was eager to hear the outcome of my meeting with the director of the memorial since we were both hoping I would get the job—we had anticipated it would be better-paying than the one I had. It was important for both of us that I get the job since she wanted us to get engaged and married as soon as possible, for fear that waiting too long would change the feelings we had for each other. In addition, we were running the risk of having premarital sex, which was contradictory to her Pentecostal faith. She also believed that her father would pray and find out that we were unchaste. As soon as I told her I had been selected as the best candidate for the job, she put on a grin.

Then in the middle of our conversation, she said, "I knew it!" with such a relief that it seemed a treasured truth was being confirmed before her eyes.

"What do you mean?" I asked.

"I knew you were not H," she replied.

"What is H?" I asked.

She laughed hard and asked, "You don't know what H means?"

"I don't know," I replied. "It could mean a lot of things," and I started imagining all kinds of words and adjectives that started with H and that were relevant to the conversation we were having, but I could not find any.

"I knew you were not Hutu," she finally exclaimed.

Then, I got startled a little and looked her in the eyes and laughed harder than she had laughed. "How do you know I am not Hutu?" I asked.

"Well...your fingers, your feet, and your pelvic girdle. Plus, they would not have offered you the job if you weren't Tutsi. I knew it already, but the fact that they gave you a job at the Kigali Genocide Memorial confirms it even further."

When I did not confirm with her that I was Tutsi, it was her turn to be startled. Things went from funny to awkward. Then she asked, "Are you Hutu?"

"No, I am not," I said. "But I am not Tutsi either."

She got even more confused, and then asked laughing, "So are you Twa?"

Jeanette meant this as a joke. The Twa are the pigmy hunter-gatherers that comprise about one percent of the Rwandan population, and are believed to have been the first inhabitants to settle in the Kingdom of Rwanda, before the arrival of the Hutus, and then the Tutsis. They have been historically marginalized, and people have made up all kinds of jokes about them. It seems that at least two jokes out of five are about Twa people. Fortunately, consciousness about their marginalization has been growing and the government discourages derogatory terms that were used to refer to them.

"So what are you?" Jeanette continued when I did not reply.

"What do you think I am?" I asked.

"I think you are Tutsi, but Jean Marie thinks I should dig more."

I laughed at this remark about her cousin and said, "Well…I consider myself human, with Rwandan citizenship. That is what I call myself and know to be true. I would encourage you to do your own research. That would actually help me know what other people think I am," I said firmly.

Part of her hoped I was joking, but the idea that she could be wrong about my identity was clearly embarrassing, awkward, and disappointing. Her face faded from happy to dejected. And then she became angry—angry that I could be so naïve about things that could jeopardize our relationship.

Then she said, even more perplexed, "So you don't know your

ethnicity? What about your father?"

"I don't know how he identifies himself. He has never told me about it, and I would not even know how to ask him. He never talks about it, and I don't care because it would not change anything about who I consider myself to be."

Jeanette was incredulous. "You're so naive. How can you not know what your ethnicity is? Ask your father. I don't know if my family would let us get married if they weren't sure about your ethnicity," she said.

"Well. If that's important for them and they can't give their daughter's hand to a person whose ethnicity is Rwando-Human, I think we should stop thinking about marriage," I remarked in a harsh tone.

Then she got angrier, and said, "So you don't want to get married anymore? You don't love me?"

"Well, I love you, but I guess we'll not get married since your family is so important to you," I said. "Why don't you ask Jean Marie to ask his family that lives near my native town what people say my father's ethnicity is?"

In the talks I used to attend about the history of the genocide, I had heard that when killers were not sure whether the person they were going to kill was Hutu or Tutsi, they could tell by examining specific physical features of the victim, and one of those features was their fingers and palms. According to the government of national unity's version, these features were not scientifically correct, and Tutsi and Hutu were socio-economic classes, not ethnic groups. But here I was being lectured by my girlfriend, who was Tutsi, about what distinguished Tutsi from Hutu. She and I had been dating for three months, during which time she had repeatedly told me how much she loved the shape of my head, my long fingers and toes, and my hip bones. She reminded me many times that we would give birth to Miss and Mister Rwanda. I was happy she liked my physique, but I had no idea she was indirectly referring to her perception that I was Tutsi.

I had met Jeannette at my friend's house. He was newly wedded and had been her high school teacher, and he and I sang in the same choir. I was paying him a visit as a courtesy required by the Rwandan culture. She asked my phone number as we parted. I texted her when I got home and told her that I was pleased to meet her. The next time we talked, she was sick, and I encouraged her to go to see the doctor, which she did not feel very enthusiastic about. When I offered to accompany her, she agreed. I took a motor taxi to Kanombe and met her at the bus stop. And we both took the bus to downtown Kigali.

She seemed a little sad about her life, and for some reason that attracted me. I felt that I could motivate her to be happier and more successful. She shared that she worked at the U.S. Embassy on a research project with the U.S. Agency for International Development (USAID), but that the contractor had not paid them for the previous three months or so. I had a job that paid me a decent salary, so I offered to help her as I could. She also went to the Kigali Institute of Management, a private college, and she paid tuition out-of-pocket with the help of her cousin Jean Marie.

When we arrived at her oculist, she learned she had to buy new glasses, but she did not have enough money to pay for them, so I offered to pay. (In the Rwandan culture, it is embarrassing for a man to be presented with a problem by a girl and fail to solve it—sexist, right?) I did not know what Jeannette's intention was when I accompanied her to her eye doctor, but I would have helped her even if we weren't dating. After I paid for her glasses, she took me to her friend's workplace. Her friend worked in a studio owned by an Indian couple, and they took all kinds of pictures including U.S. visa photos. Her friend encouraged us to take a picture together, so we did. I sat on a stool and she sat on my lap. We smiled at the photographer and he took two wallet-size pictures that each of us carried in our wallets. From that day, there was no question as to whether we were dating or not. Our relationship grew fast.

Jeanette passed by my office on her way back from work, and we hung out until as late as 10:00 p.m. We did not notice time passing by, and usually I would walk her to Remera Bus Station to catch the bus to Kanombe. In retrospect, we were two infatuated, co-dependent lovers. I would go home and text her to find out whether she had made it home safely. Before we both went to bed we talked for at least two or three hours—sometimes until 2:00 a.m., even when we both had to wake up early and go to work. In the morning, we texted or called each other and talked about how we'd thought or dreamt about each other for the three hours of sleep we had. And of course, we would talk about how much we missed each other. On weekends, she came to visit me in Kimironko.

After that awkward lunch in Nyabugogo, we took a bus together. On the bus, Jeanette insisted that I should ask my father what ethnicity my family was. I repeated to her that I would not know how to start that conversation with my father since he never talked to us about the ethnic divides in Rwanda. "We relate to all people regardless of their background," I said to her.

I told her that I was in Rwanda when the genocide happened but was not targeted by the Interahamwe militia. I did not tell her that my mother had disappeared in the Democratic Republic of Congo when the refugee camps were invaded by the Rwanda Defense Force and Laurent Desire Kabila's rebels. Neither did I tell her that I had survived killings by the RPA in Rwanda, during which my grandfather was killed in front of my eyes. I thought that would be too much truth for her to handle in just one day.

However, I did share with her that the fact that my family was not targeted by killers, when Tutsis were being murdered, had made me suspect that we could be Hutu. The thought of possibly sharing an ethnic identity with the radicals who orchestrated such a horrific genocide caused me much shame and guilt.

I once heard from my sisters that my paternal uncle Rudoviko told them our family was Tutsi who had changed their identity cards in the 1950s for fear of being persecuted. At the time, that made me feel a little bit of relief to know that at least I did not share the same genes with Hutus; however, I did not have any tangible proof other than my physical features that matched those of the Tutsi, according to how I heard people describe me.

I'd also had a few instances where Tutsis approached me and warned me against talking to Hutus. One of them was an adult student named Jeanne, to whom I taught English while I was in college. Her family fled to Tanzania in 1959 during the Hutu revolution when thousands of Tutsis were forced into exile. Jeanne was a good friend in addition to being my English student. I did not know why she had become closer to me than any other students in her class until she shared with me that she liked me and Christopher—another student of mine—because we were imfura, a word that originally meant "a person of integrity" but that somehow took on another meaning: Tutsi. I must admit that I was not courageous enough at that time to tell her that I wasn't Tutsi, but just Rwandan, a national identity I decided to adopt to remain neutral in the ethnic conflicts that had culminated in the Rwandan genocide.

Another good friend with whom I could not share my radical rejection of ethnic identification was a primary school teacher whom I met in the Rulindo district in the Northern Province, where I was training teachers to use English as a medium of instruction. This was in 2009, after the government decided to change away from French as the official language of instruction. He had invited me to his home after school and warned me against socializing with the other teachers that were in my class because they were Hutu. I understood his lack of trust because he had gone through horrible experiences and lost many members of his family, but at the same time, I knew the country could not move forward if there remained so much mistrust among its people. I was of a different generation and felt I had a responsibility to restore trust and unity, so I continued to interact with all the teachers equally.

I had not been bold enough to share with my two friends my chosen identity of being just Rwandan and human above all, but I was determined to share it with my girlfriend now that she was starting to talk about marriage. I had resolved that my children would not inherit the ethnic divides that tore my country apart, and I expected my girlfriend and potential future wife to share the same resolve. This was non-negotiable.

One day after our awkward conversation about ethnicity, I stopped by the Tigo vendors sitting under the green, blue, and white umbrellas outside the Remera bus station, to buy minutes for my phone. A woman I did not know told me, "Your relationship with the girl you are buying minutes to talk to is not healthy for you." I did not know the woman, and I do not believe she knew me either. But her statement rang true. My relationship with Jeanette had become more and more co-dependent, and I suspected she liked me because I could support her financially. I was helping her with college tuition, and she asked for more money to give her family when she traveled back to the Eastern Province to visit with them. I had seen too many red flags to just continue the relationship.

I painfully invited Jeanette to a restaurant and amicably broke up with her. Jeanette was so upset that she refused to return the camera she had borrowed from me—a gift I had received from my Hawaiian friends when I visited Oahu in 2011. That is when I learned to follow the signs and to say no, even to people whom I loved, as long as I meant it. I was so naïve and had little experience dating, and Jeanette was my first serious relationship. I was so afraid to hurt her feelings that if it hadn't been for the many signs I saw, including the intercession of the lady at the Tigo vendors, I would never have gathered the courage to terminate the relationship. I was too nice then, like a good seminarian.

From Trauma to Peace

As we sat on the green shore of Lake Muhazi in eastern Rwanda, my colleague Diana asked, "You have been interviewing all these people with us, would you like to share your reflections on camera?"

It was 2013, and I had been working on a project for four years with the Thought Field Therapy Foundation to treat trauma and other psychological problems. They decided to document the success stories of the participants, and I was offered a position as a translator and a co-interviewer for the documentary. Now, Diana was inviting me to be a subject in the film.

"Maybe," I replied.

Initially, I was not supposed to be interviewed in the film, but Diana thought I could tie the story together as a Rwandan who had followed the project since its inception. I was hesitant since the other interpreter who had tried to share his story on camera jeopardized the project because he shared that he survived the genocide, while his mother died in 1994 in Byumba. He shied away from naming the RPA as the army responsible for his mother's death and simply called it "genocide." (Many people who were in Rwanda in 1994 still use the term "genocide" to mean the genocide against the Tutsi *and* the RPF war, collectively. For those who survived RPA war crimes, it is a way to be vague so they don't explicitly name the RPA as aggressors and risk getting in trouble.) Sadly, my other Rwandan colleagues who knew this interpreter and his history well were afraid his story would jeopardize the project, and they asked the American videographer to omit it from the documentary, since it would be dangerous for him, and for all of us, if the story got out.

I thought about Diana's invitation for a few minutes and agreed to be interviewed. The interviews I had helped conduct with genocide survivors had unburied my own genocide traumas, but I felt strong enough to give the interview. Furthermore, I felt a responsibility to help tell the stories of people who had been generous and trusting enough to welcome me into their homes and their lives in the aftermath of the violence. And I knew what was politically correct and safe to say about the genocide. "I should be able to stay away from controversial areas," I thought.

Bob, the videographer, quickly found a spot, and the camera rolled. It was only my second time ever being filmed, and I had never publicly discussed my experiences in the genocide. I wanted to represent the best of Rwanda, and I thought I could put my personal grievances aside and speak to the people who had trusted the Thought Field Therapy Foundation with their stories. I had co-interviewed them without ever sharing my own story, and I wanted to change that.

"In what ways has this project transformed you?" Diana began.

"Being Rwandan itself, being part of a country that has gone through the worst genocide in the world, a country that has become synonymous with genocide, a country where sixty percent of the population is poor, it affects me. But knowing that people are healing, lots of people are starting small businesses after healing from trauma, people are finding back their lives, is refreshing and makes me proud of being Rwandan."

"What do you want the world to know about Rwanda?" she continued.

I had never had to speak for my country, and my mind completely shifted; I found myself transcending from the part (a citizen) to the whole (the Rwandan people). The stories of healing and hope I had heard at the Thought Field Therapy Foundation—from people like Verena, who had lived with trauma for fifty years, lost her entire family, adopted thirteen children, and was only able to heal and smile after she was treated with Thought Field Therapy; and like Colette, who was able to forgive her parents' killer after finding healing—had given me optimism. I channeled that feeling as I spoke to Diana, saying:

> I would like the world to see Rwanda as a country,
> As a people,
> A strong people,
> A people that can overcome anything,
> A people that has gone through the worst thing
> you can imagine,
> And was able to recover from it.
> A country that is rebuilding,
> A people that forgives,
> A people that reconciles,
> A people that wants to set an example to the

world,
An example of how you can overcome a conflict,
develop a strong economy, and unify a people.
I would like the world to know that we are one
people,
That we have the same feelings, the same
aspirations.
If one person has a problem, it is everybody's
problem.
So, I would like the world to always stick together.
We are *all* in this war together,
The war to fight poverty,
to fight conflicts,
to fight trauma,
to fight human trafficking,
And all these issues we keep seeing recurring in
the news,
We are all in this together and together we can
make the world a better place.

The camera stopped rolling, and I could not believe that I had such passion inside me. I had never voiced my hopes for Rwanda before, and when I agreed to the interview, I did not anticipate how talking with Diana would reopen my old wounds. It was an emotionally tense experience, but I was glad I did it. I do not know what Diana anticipated, but I knew she was pleased with the interview, and so was Bob.

That documentary let me give the world my message, and it inspired in me a desire to write about my personal journey, which would take more than just a three-minute interview. My greatest struggle would be to find balance between telling the collective, hopeful story of the country's recovery and the story of unaddressed horror I had survived at the hands of those associated with the current ruling party and rebuilders of my native land.

Inclusive Commemoration

*Fear of freedom, of which its possessor is not necessarily
aware, makes him see ghosts. Such an individual is actually
taking refuge in an attempt to achieve security, which he or
she prefers to the risks of liberty.*

—Paulo Freire

For twenty-one years, I hoped the RPF would come out
and apologize for the crimes that some of their members had
committed against innocent civilians, including my grandfather and cousin. I understood that genocide crimes had to be
punished first, and that genocide survivors needed time to heal,
and so did the country as a whole; but I also needed to heal like a
citizen with equal rights.

Unfortunately the government of Rwanda continued to
accuse those who mentioned crimes committed by RPA soldiers
of espousing the Hutu Power ideology and denying the genocide.
To be fair, some people did deny the genocide and they should
be held accountable for that; but I started to realize that my own
story could easily be politicized and considered genocide denial.

Today, after studying political science, I understand that many politicians play any cards at their disposal to silence those who willingly or unwillingly undermine their legitimacy. But I was not a politician and did not intend to tarnish anybody's image. I just wanted to tell my story. I wanted to put my piece of the puzzle on the table, hoping that it would contribute to understanding the intricate story of Rwanda. I felt a responsibility to share my story and contribute to what I regarded as the incomplete official narrative about the genocide. I knew I would regret not being brave enough to tell my story if I did not take the chance.

I was also old enough to realize that until I made peace with the life-changing experiences I had lived through as a child, I could not heal. I was heartbroken for myself and for my people. I felt a big hole in my heart that needed to be filled. I worried about not being able to connect with my friends, since I could not share with them some of my most troubling secrets. I felt excluded from the national story, and sometimes it sounded like I was being lumped in with everyone who had committed or supported the genocide. To make things worse, no one seemed to talk about what I had experienced. Was it irrelevant? Was it not part of the Rwandan story? I felt like Rwanda was a story in which I could not find my character. I felt non-Rwandan. I felt ignored. Excluded. I loved Rwanda, but it seemed like Rwanda did not care about me. I empathized with others, but no one empathized with me. And even though I had grown to love and accept myself, I started feeling like my traumas did not matter; that my deceased family did not deserve sympathy; that somehow I deserved death and witnessing my loved ones being murdered in front of my own eyes.

I realized that if I had agaciro (a sense of self-worth), I had to challenge the danger of a single and simplistic story. If my beloved ones also mattered, I had to exhume their stories, even if it meant confronting those who celebrated their deaths and my suffering. But most importantly, I had to help my country heal. I believed I could use my story to share my side of the story and hopefully help Rwandans pay more attention to the untold stories, to the uncomforted hearts, to the undried tears.

In 2013, as I was working with a local peace-building organization, the topic of inclusive commemoration came up as the twenty-year anniversary of the genocide approached. My colleagues and I were preparing genocide commemoration activities, and one of our aims was to encourage young people from all backgrounds to participate in commemoration activities. When a German colleague brought this goal to the executive secretary, who was Rwandan, he stated that inclusive commemoration meant everyone had the obligation to commemorate the genocide against the Tutsi. I was crestfallen. For me, inclusive meant that we would commemorate *all* lives lost during the 100-day genocide, during the war, and in the aftermath.

I did not share my point of view since I knew it was not politically correct to include lives that were taken by some RPA soldiers. I knew some people had raised the issue and ended up in prison with allegations of inciting violence, so I kept quiet and smiled. It was an awkward conversation to have, and I wondered what inclusive commemoration meant to my German colleague; but it seemed she was familiar enough with the situation to know the organization was not ready to start the conversation about RPA war crimes. She did not share her opinion, either, and we both agreed to follow the interpretation of our boss.

I must say I empathized with my boss. There was an official narrative that even the civil society could not challenge as they pleased. In fact, it was hard to know the right thing to say, so one had to stay as far away from controversy as possible.

During the genocide commemoration, I was bothered by the idea that my grandfather and cousin were not among the victims the government wanted Rwandans to mourn, even though they were killed during the 100 days. I privately resolved that I did not need the government to validate whether their lives were worth commemorating, so I decided that I would go to commemoration events and remember all the victims of the genocide against the Tutsi, and also my grandfather, cousin, mother, Kennedy, Abimana, and everyone who I knew died from April to July 1994, and before and after. I did not have to tell anyone that my personal commemoration included every Rwandan life that perished from 1959 to 1994, and after.

I was still ruminating the idea of writing my story, but the danger associated with the act kept proving real. More and more people who tried to bring up crimes committed by the RPA, whether implicitly or explicitly, faced grave consequences. The most notorious victim would be Kizito Mihigo, an artist who started the eponymous Kizito Mihigo Peace Foundation to promote peace and reconciliation through music. He was a Tutsi genocide survivor who carried out countrywide peace-building campaigns, including in prisons. His songs were the most popular music that aired during the genocide commemoration. Then, one weekend in April 2014, he disappeared after releasing a song on YouTube entitled "Igisobanuro Cy'urupfu" (The Meaning of Death), in which he said that even though he was a survivor of the genocide against the Tutsi, he also commemorated the deaths of those who perished in other killings that were not called genocide. The lyrics read, in part:

> Though the genocide orphaned me,
> let it not make me lose empathy for others.

Their lives too were brutally taken
but not qualified as genocide.
Those brothers and sisters
they too are human beings.
I pray for them.
I comfort them.
I remember them
Death is never good,
be it by the genocide, or war,
or slaughtered in revenge killings.

By acknowledging other killings that were not termed "geno-cide," Kizito Mihigo implicitly alluded to crimes the RPA had committed, which some people (mainly the diaspora opposi-tion) had tried to call another "genocide." After a few days, the police admitted they had him in custody on charges of conspiring against the government of Rwanda, and he remained imprisoned until 2018. The incident shocked everybody, for Kizito Mihigo was regarded as a peaceful patriot, and pro-RPF. His song would not be played on any radio station, whether public or private.

(At the time of this book's publication, I learned that Kizito Mihigo has passed on. He is believed to have been tortured and murdered by the Rwandan government in his prison cell. His songs continue to comfort Rwandans and inspire those laboring for genuine apolitical truth and reconciliation of ALL Rwandans.)

After these events, I knew I could not contemplate writing my story in Rwanda. The RPF was not yet ready to start the conversation about revenge killings against innocent civilians. Kizito Mihigo's arrest confirmed for me that speaking out as a survivor or a witness to crimes committed by the former military wing of the current ruling party could be fatal.

I faced two choices: stay in Rwanda and keep my mouth shut, or leave the country and write my story with the risk of never returning to my native land. The cost was very high, but I could not fight my nature. Surviving crimes and being prevented from talking about them was unbearable. It was worse than dying.

I did not have much time to think about it because I was supposed to travel to the U.S. in two months. I had a ten-year visa, and Bob, the videographer I worked with on the documentary film, lived in Hawaii. I was supposed to travel to his home to do the final editing of the film with him for two weeks. After that, I did not know what I was going to do. I did not know Bob well enough to involve him in what I had come to regard as my permanent escape. I knew I was not going back to Rwanda, but I did not know where I was going to stay.

The one thing I did know for certain was that freedom and healing were as important to me as eating or breathing. I knew I needed to tell my story to heal from the wounds of a tragic past and a traumatic childhood. I did not want any form of justice other than to tell my story. I did not want anyone punished for the crimes I survived, but I reserved the right to tell my story, and I was willing to pay any price to do just that. Furthermore, I was certain this was the right thing to do not just for myself, but for my mother, my grandfather, and my cousin. It was the right thing to do for my country. I was convinced that my country needed *truth* more than anything else. I could not see how a country could heal without *truth*.

I could not let anyone stop me from fulfilling this strong sense of responsibility to tell the truth about the crimes I had survived and witnessed as a child. And so, I made my decision to leave Rwanda, for good, without letting anyone know my full intentions, including my father. I would leave behind *everything*. My home. My career. Family. Friends.

All that I took with me were memories.

Coming to America

Two weeks before my flight, I met a friend of mine, Annon-ciata, who had worked with me in the Peace Corps in 2011. She was in my neighborhood, visiting with her sister's family. I told her I was going to leave the country and that I did not plan to return for a while, but I did not give her details as to why I was going. I had heard stories of people who had helped Rwandans to flee the country being persecuted, and I did not wish to leave her life in danger.

As if she knew that I did not have anyone to host me after my planned two-week stint in Hawaii, she told me she had a sister who lived in Maine. She said she would ask her sister to host me for a few days if I needed a place to stay. It was my first confir-mation that everything would be taken care of if I trusted in the process.

About a week prior to my departure, I traveled to my home-town to visit my family and bid them farewell. I did not want to involve them in my escape in any way, so I only told them that I was going to the U.S. for work and that I intended to stay there after my job concluded to look for graduate school opportunities. I tried to conceal my sadness, but deep inside I knew I might never see them again.

Early in the morning, I left my home and took the bus back to Kigali to prepare for a one-way trip to the U.S. I looked through the window of the bus like I did the first time I went to Kigali as a child; but this time I knew it was not the banana trees moving backwards, and that I was the one moving on the bus, leaving my family, and my roots, knowing that I might never see them again. For the first time, I wished I had visited my family more often. I was proud of my roots and had gotten over the stigma of coming from the countryside.

As my town disappeared behind me in the rearview mirror of the bus, I thought back over all the happy childhood adventures I had had. The bus drove past Zaza parish, where I had gone to mass every Sunday as a child, and on Fridays as a seminarian.

We stopped at the corner of Zaza Primary School, where I had gone to school and played soccer barefoot, to pick up passengers. To our left was the Teacher Training College, where my father had taught, where I played volleyball when I was in high school, and where I watched handball games every Sunday as a child. Next to the college was the Cultural Center, where I had gone to read the rare comic books and play with hula-hoops and other toys that we could not make ourselves. As the bus moved away, I realized that I was leaving behind the place that I called home and that had shaped my childhood and adolescence. But, when we passed Kanazi, the hill where I was separated from my parents and where I jumped a corpse as I fled the deafening rain of bullets, I realized that I was leaving not only the places that held good memories, but also those that held my traumas.

Suddenly, a bittersweet feeling gusted through my whole body. For the first time, I had an opportunity to go away from all the places that triggered all these feelings—bad and good—and look back at them from a distance. I had a chance to revisit my traumas, make peace with the past, and move on. But most importantly, I could now contemplate the idea of telling my story and name the perpetrators without the fear of being forcibly disappeared, or the worry of rotting in prison.

As my plane's departure time approached at the airport, I developed a fear that I might be prevented from boarding. I thought about all the times I had been critical of the regime, or mentioned the crimes I had survived, and I started imagining all sorts of people who might have spied on me. Granted, those times were few. In Rwanda, people said that everybody spied on everybody so it was imprudent to mention anything that could upset the ruling elite—to anyone. The fear of the RPF was so intense that we thought that they even read our minds. Even my closest friends did not know about what I had been through, and I knew it was dangerous to share anything with them lest I put them in danger, or risk losing them as friends. I had only told my story to two friends whom I knew well, and I was almost certain they would not report me unless they were forced to.

On the day of my departure, these friends and few others accompanied me to the airport, as is the tradition. I bid them farewell and went through security. I tried to conceal my fear when the airport staff asked me many questions about the purpose of my trip to Hawaii. It felt like someone knew about my secret plan and wanted to sabotage it. Although they let me go through the terminal without incident, I did not believe I was safe until I landed on U.S. soil. As I landed at Kahului airport, I sighed in relief. I was free. After concluding my work in Maui, I flew to Maine, which would become my second home.

The American Dream:
The Price of Freedom

It is solely by risking life that freedom is obtained...
the individual who has not staked his or her life may, no
doubt, be recognized as a Person; but he or she has not
attained the truth of this recognition as an
independent self-consciousness.

—Georg Hegel

As my Somali driver pulled into my host family's driveway at 74 Birch Street, Lewiston, Maine, I was shocked by the level of poverty I saw around me: old wooden houses with dusty carpets; Somali kids wandering the streets named after trees. This was nothing like the America I had imagined.

I had called my host family before taking the cab, but my host mother did not answer the phone. I knew no one else in Maine, so I had no choice but to go to the address and hope all would be well. I paid my driver $80 as we had agreed at the Portland airport and headed upstairs to the second floor, where my host family lived. I knocked on the door of the second apartment, and no one answered.

I had spent almost all the money I had on my flight and only had $200 left. I knocked a second time, and a third time, but no one answered the door. I did not have a local phone number so I decided to open the door. As soon as I entered, I heard the noise of someone taking a shower in the bathroom.

"My host mother must be taking a shower," I thought. I called out my greetings, and thankfully she responded. It was the right apartment!

When she was done taking a shower, she greeted me and welcomed me to her humble dwelling. She and her family would become my first American family.

I had to apply for asylum in one year, as required by the Department of Homeland Security. Otherwise my application would be invalid. It was one of the most difficult choices I had ever made. I knew it would take a long time before I could get a green card and start traveling, which meant I would not be able to return to my country any time soon.

The risks involved in ever going back to my country were high, but seeking refuge in the U.S., based on the fact that it was unsafe for me to tell my story in Rwanda, was not without its own costs. I knew many professors, lawyers, and journalists who could no longer travel back to Rwanda because they had been critical of the government. If I was going to do what I was convinced was my mission of being a voice of unity and forgiveness, I would inevitably have to address all the crimes committed in 1994 and afterward, despite the immensity of the danger. I might never be allowed back in my country.

Furthermore, my whole family still lived in Rwanda, and I

did not know what the consequences of sharing my story would mean for their safety. I had heard stories of families of government critics living abroad being harassed. Though my intention was not to criticize the government but to tell my own story, I knew that doing so would not be well received by the Rwandan government, so I feared for my family's wellbeing and mourned the thought that I might not be able to see them or even talk to them again.

I pondered my options day and night, but I knew it was increasingly dangerous for me to go back to my country since I was becoming more vocal about the crimes I had survived, and I knew the risks could amount to prison or forced disappearance. I also knew that I could not live the rest of my life in fear that those whose image risked being tarnished by my story would attempt to terminate my life. To be clear, I never considered any form of opposition or revenge, but I knew I couldn't stay silent anymore. I'd had a relatively comfortable life in Rwanda, but that was not fulfilling to me. I could not heal without the freedom to tell my story, without finding time to process what I had gone through in the genocide and war. I strongly felt that I owed a debt to my grandfather and cousin to tell the story of their deaths and so many other innocent lives that had been slaughtered in cold blood.

In Rwanda, every time I passed the military patrolling the streets of Kigali at 4:00 p.m., I could not stop thinking that they were associated with the same soldiers who killed my grandfather and cousin, and possibly my mother. Though I bore no animosity towards them as individuals, they triggered traumatic memories of the crimes I had survived. Those memories were with me still in Maine, and every single day I would ask myself whether my choice was worth the risk. I started developing a fear of communicating with my family regularly, as if to prepare them and myself for the possibility of not being able to stay in touch. In retrospect, I believe my withdrawal from them was mostly for myself; I had to train myself to love my family without seeing them, or even communicating with them. I did the same with my friends in Rwanda to protect them. Ultimately, I decided I would leave the line of communication open as long as I was not talking about anything that could put them in danger. At least before I published my story, I would stay in touch with them, but I would not tell them I had fled my country. My conscience was clear that I had not committed any crime, nor sought anyone's demise, so I thought I would leave my friends the choice to decide how to relate to me—a decision that I knew could change the more I shared about myself. Surely, for example, my friends who thought I had survived the genocide against the Tutsis like they had, and had confessed to me their resentment towards Hutus, would look at me differently.

"Would they still be my friends after I call their heroes my villains?" I worried. "Would they look at me the same way?"

Not only would I disclose that the soldiers of the Rwandan Patriotic Army were responsible for the crimes I had survived, I would also go public that I had fled my country—the two scariest and most dangerous things a Rwandan can ever disclose. Even Rwandans living in the diaspora would be more likely to distance themselves from me for fear that they could be labeled anti-RPF by association—a label that no Rwandan wanted stamped on them. I risked losing everything that was familiar.

As for my host family, they were Rwandans who had fled the persecution of Tutsis in 1959 by the first Hutu Republic, lived in Congo for three decades, and could only now return to Rwanda after the RPA won the war and took power. The Rwanda Patriotic

Army that almost killed me, and that took the life of my grandfather and three-year-old cousin, were their heroes.

To make the situation even more awkward, my host mother always told me what a typical Tutsi I was, with my long legs and neck. Just like her sister who had introduced me to her, she had assumed I survived the crimes committed by Hutu extremists in 1994. How would I tell her that the Kagame-led RPA was responsible for my tragic childhood trauma? Would she still call me son? She was very fond of Kagame mainly because he was from the Abega clan, and because he had led the rebellion that allowed her family to return to Rwanda.

But my insurmountable yearning to live a truthful life and share my story was greater than my longing for acceptance and approval. I bore no animosity towards my friends, in fact I loved them dearly, so I had nothing to feel badly about; but I was always suspicious they loved me for the wrong reasons.

PART II

THE ABYSS OF HOPE

*My Journey to Healing,
Forgiveness, Truth, Love,
Peace, and Joy*

Freedom and Healing

Freedom is what you do with what's been done to you.
—Jean-Paul Sartre

It is by going down into the abyss that we recover the treasures of life. Where you stumble, there lies your treasure.
—Joseph Campbell

The wound is the place where the Light enters you.
—Rumi

My healing journey has involved no professional psycho-therapy, though I did try Thought Field Therapy, a tapping therapy that uses acupressure points. It is highly possible that this therapy helped me heal emotions associated with my trau-matic experiences as I dove into hell to face all my demons and arose with triumphant joy and fearlessness. Ultimately, I have engaged in an intellectual and spiritual inner battle with the *truth*, a deep meditation and reflection done with the utmost detachment, but mostly driven by a *genuine* search for healing, meaning, peace, and the solutions to the tragedy I survived and witnessed.

It was meditation and introspection that deepened my healing through a reinterpretation of my story. This process helped me see myself not as a victim, but as a warrior. The work of thinkers like Don Miguel Ruiz and Paul Ferrini helped cement my new belief system, which contributed a great deal to my healing. But above all, it was writing my story that truly healed me. I took back my power to craft the story I told myself about myself. Coming up with a narrative of what I had been through brought more clarity to my life. It helped me understand how I became *me*. I became the author of my story and understood that how I interpreted experiences I had lived mattered.

This journey would start at the dusty desktop computers of Tree Street Youth Center, the after-school program in Lewiston, Maine, where I volunteered as I waited for my work authorization and social security clearance so I could start working legally in the United States. My friend Jake had prompted me to open a Pandora's box of memories when I hesitantly said yes to that interview for his podcast. It was the morning after sharing a longer version of my survival story with Jake that I embarked on my writing journey, at 4:00 a.m. on a chilly Maine winter morning. After that point, there was no going back or stroking my wounds. I knew I would have to open them with the scalpel of truth, and heal them with love and forgiveness. That was the only way I knew to deal with any problem: get to the bottom of it.

I wrote the first chapters of my life story, pertaining to my childhood, at Tree Street Youth Center in the winter of 2015. For some time, I avoided dealing with the most traumatic chapters of my life, which involved facing death and losing my mother. I finally got the courage to write about them during my internship with the Africa Center for Strategic Studies in Washington, D.C. the following year. On weekends and after work, I would take a chair to Rock Creek Park in Georgetown, where I lived at the time. I sat by the creek and purged my painful memories into a Microsoft Word document.

Nature and solitude were my refuge during my writing process. The sound of water making its way through rocks, and rapids clashing against rocks, cleansed my soul and washed away my sorrows. The clean air from green trees rejuvenated me with new life and aloha.

I traveled around the U.S. and connected with wonderful people and the country as my writing journey continued: from the Forks, Maine; to Rock Creek Park and the Potomac River in Washington, D.C.; to Southern California; and Florence, Oregon. I wrote the last chapters of my story in Sedona, Arizona after I completed my graduate degree at the School of Policy and International Affairs at the University of Maine. I took a few months off to finish the manuscript of this book during the winter of 2017/2018.

At the Bourbon Coffee Shop on Pennsylvania Avenue in Washington, D.C., I soothed my nostalgia for home as I re-rewrote this book. I contemplated with awe the walls adorned with Imigongo paintings and Rwandan baskets, sipped Rwandan coffee, and enjoyed the Rwandan music that played in the background, sometimes listening to Corneille Nyungura's music with my headphones when the coffee shop got louder.

The following pages hold insights I gained during lengthy conversations with myself in all of those places, on the shores of

Rock Creek, Oak Creek, and the Kennebec River, and in my dark room between four and six in the morning. I now open those conversations to you.

Grieving and Honoring
My Mother

My mother left a vacuum in my family that no one can fill. She was a strong, take-charge woman and also an extremely loving human being. Those who lived with her for two years in a refugee camp in Congo have shared that she never recovered from her separation from my sister, Lily, my brother, Valery, and me. I don't think we ever recovered from her loss either. We waited for her from the day my father, Thierry, and Kiki returned to Rwanda, but she never came back.

Occasionally, we would hear that someone had spotted a woman who looked like her among the returnees to our town, but then we would end up hearing that it wasn't her. One day we heard that she was in Gitarama, which is about three hours from our town. My father took a trip to go find her. We hoped he would come back with her, but he would find that what we had heard were mere rumors. We heard news from other people we had known who were still in Congo, but no one mentioned that they had seen her.

For five, ten, fifteen years we waited, and we finally came to peace with the idea that she might be dead. But of course, we had not seen her body and did not know the circumstances in which she had died, so it was hard to completely accept her death and have closure. We did not talk about her much around the house except that, occasionally, we went to Mass on the feast day of her patron saint, Saint Bazilissa, in her honor. Other people who had lost their loved ones would request a mass to pray for them. But we never did because we didn't know whether she had died or not.

On more than one occasion, I saw a woman who looked like her from a distance and hurried to catch up with her, only to get closer and realize it was someone else. I imagined all sorts of stories about what might have happened to her in the Congolese jungle, plagued as it was by atrocities of all sorts. Was she killed by the Rwandan Patriotic Army, turned Rwandan Defense Force, during the raids on refugee camps? Or did she survive, only to be abducted by FDLR or other rebel groups in Congo? Did they kill her or did they force her into marriage? What about Petite, my youngest sister she carried on her back? Did she live or die? Every story about the suffering of women in the areas controlled by rebel groups in Congo could be my mother's story. Twenty-five years later, I don't know how to respond to those who ask about my mother.

Her absence was felt the most on Christmas Day. When she was still physically with us, she made mandazi (donuts), cooked feast meals for at least two days, and bought everybody new clothes. In Rwanda, when you have a party, you are supposed to invite everybody you know, especially your family, friends, and neighbors. Even those who are not invited can attend your party, and it is considered rude to ask them to leave or to tell them that you don't have anything to offer them to drink. When you are wealthy, those who are less wealthy will expect to have a better, free meal or beer at your party, and they won't usually bring anything to the party.

My mother, knowing that many people would show up to our house on Christmas Day, prepared a lot of food, and our house, backyard, and front yard were full of people. Some close friends and relatives would even sit in some of our bedrooms, except our parents' bedroom. On Christmas Eve, we borrowed chairs and benches from our neighbors, and since we did not know how many guests to expect even on the very day of Christmas, we would continue to borrow more chairs as we ran out of seats.

My father's name was Noël (Christmas), which perhaps helps account for how very many neighbors stopped by our house and asked for Christmas beer or food. Most people assumed that my father's birthday was on Christmas Day. I also thought that it was his birthday, but I would later learn that it wasn't. Growing up we never celebrated birthdays. Not many people did. Now my father celebrates his birthday, or rather, his friends remind him of his birthday and give him presents. It wasn't until I started middle school that I started celebrating birthdays—I suspect because of the influence of globalization.

It was in my early adolescence, after middle school, that I missed my mother the most. But I also felt her spiritual presence, and I still do today. For she had not died. Even after I stopped waiting for her to miraculously show up in my life, I knew she was there spiritually. I looked for insights from my culture and religion to best honor her, but death was not a topic that many people wanted to discuss. No one had seen her body, so I could not confirm, for a fact, that she was dead. But at the same time, no one had heard news of her, so it was not possible to prove she was alive. I was Catholic, but I was doubtful about the idea of life after death. However, it was hard for me to imagine that life simply stopped after physical death. I knew that a human being was more than just a physical body. I could not believe that her spiritual self, her soul and spirit, would also die, but I wasn't sure of anything. This would normally create confusion, but somehow it started making sense to me. I stopped focusing on what I did not know and instead dwelt on what I knew and tried to reconcile the unknown, the known, and my doubts:

I knew that my mother loved me and worried about me immensely.

I also knew that she wasn't with me physically, whether dead or afar.

I was aware that she wanted me to be happy, respectful, and successful, so I decided that, at that age, doing well in school, and staying out of trouble was the best way I could honor her.

Somehow I understood that a mother who was away from her children worried the most, so I decided I would not make my mother worry about me, especially when she could not be there for me.

I decided I would make sure that wherever she was, she would be at peace knowing that her son was behaving as if she were around.

I had no doubt in mind that it was the right thing to do, so it wasn't hard to follow through. I was not the most studious or well-behaved of all the kids, but I knew my boundaries. I did not pass all my school assignments but when I failed one, I knew not to fail a second one. I fell in love with girls and became obsessed with the female body like any other straight teenaged boy, but I knew not to take advantage of women or hurt them. I liked parties, and I drank sometimes but I knew I should not get drunk or do drugs. I did not possess the most fortitude, and sometimes I lost motivation, but somehow I managed to pick myself up and find a reason to do well in life, and to love others unconditionally.

My mother's love was ever-present in many mothers who called me "son," even before they knew I did not have my biological mother. I had lived with my mother for only eight years, physically, but she gave me all the love I needed to love myself and others unconditionally for the rest of my life; and when I thought I did not have enough love to share, somehow she refilled my heart with abundant love for myself, and then more to share with others.

On the following pages is a letter I wrote to her recently, in an attempt to express my feelings.

A Love Letter to My Mother

Dear Mom,

I miss you. So much. It's been two and a half decades since I physically saw you. I feel your presence every day. I have been strengthened by your love every step of my journey in this physical life. Thank you for sending your angels my way. They have taken good care of, cherished, and nourished me. They call me son, and treat me as such. They have provided me with many of the things you would have hoped me to get.

I feel your absence too, sometimes. I love you and promise you not to make you worry and you can count on me to do just that. I sometimes stumble and fall, but I always pick myself up, dust myself off, and keep moving. Your rebellious genes keep me active and fighting.

I am a warrior. Always fighting the good fight. The same fight I know you would be fighting. I'm sobbing at the thought of how much I have received. Unending joy, love, and prosperity of heart and soul. I promise you I will always remember you. I will not hate. Not even those who might be associated with whoever took your physical presence from me. I know that is what you want.

I miss you on Christmas. *A lot*. I am sitting on this rock by Oak Creek as I write you. The sound of water flowing, and splashing against the rocks is cleansing my sorrows and rejuvenating me with joyful energy.

I miss your mandazi and ubugali. Your garlic and thyme seasoned dishes.

I heard that in the refugee camp, you couldn't stop worrying about my siblings and me who had stayed in Rwanda. I know the thought of our absence was devastating. I love you so much, and I know you are proud of me—and that keeps me going.

I'm at peace now. I am not afraid to exhume your story and those of our loved ones who passed on. I know the risks, but it was my decision and I hope you support me.

If you don't, I understand, but your stubborn genes can't let me do otherwise. I will be fine and I assure you that my intentions will always be reconciliatory and non-blaming. I love my country and its people. All of them, without exception, just like you.

I miss our house, and all the plants we grew, and the animals we raised. I miss the banana room. I miss how Dad used to play the guitar to us as we waited for dinner to be ready. How you reminded me to do my homework. But you know what I don't miss? Your knuckles! But I have forgiven you for all the corporal punishments. I understand that you wanted me to turn out good, and I know your mother had to raise all of you by herself after Grandpa left her for his second wife.

I am grateful for your passion. Your fire. Your rebelliousness. Your loathing for hypocrisy and your love for authenticity.

Since the last time we saw each other, I have grown into a man. I have done well in school and life has blessed me with abundant love and joy, with a global army of friends and family.

I miss my father too. He has done an outstanding job raising us without your physical presence. I clashed with him a few times during my early adolescent years, but I love him, and will continue to love him even more. He has been very gentle with me and my siblings. Since you left us, he has not laid a hand on any of us, except a few times when we hurt other kids physically. He sat me down and consulted with me when I did wrong. Even when he knew I was wrong, he gave me the benefit of the doubt. He gave me a voice. He never patronized me. He told me I was going to school for my own benefit, not to please him or take care of him when he got older. That was the best advice he gave me, in addition to reminding me that if he had a job, it did not mean I had a job. I do not know how he took us to school but he did. When I saw his salary history after I obtained a government student loan, I cried; I could not believe how meager his salary was after teaching for four decades. I was making more money, working part-time as a college student. I forgave him for all the times I had thought he did not buy me new shoes. I am sobbing as I edit this letter in my apartment in Washington, D.C. two decades later, less than a mile from Capitol Hill and the White House. In America, Mom! Can you imagine? The love of your life is still wise, principled, and gentle. He is my role model, but you are my role model when it comes to speaking up. Yes! I got your rebellious genes in me also. I am half Dad, half you.

He knew I missed you, so he has learned to provide me with the tenderness you would have wanted me to feel. He has paid for our tuition, miraculously, and he has been vulnerable enough to let us know he also missed you. He missed you so much. He told us he will never love any other woman as much as he loved you. He never remarried, and I worry that he might age alone. But he is a strong and secure man.

He still loves to sing. He still walks home with a song on his lips to announce his arrival. He directs a local choir, and his choir mates surprise him on his birthday. He looks happy, but I worry about him sometimes. He loves God and prays unceasingly. I think that helps him to get through life.

He still loves sweet potatoes and hates ugali. He says ugali has no nutrients. He is still the principled rational man you married. I think he won the ugali debate. It does not have enough nutrients.

My siblings also turned out great. Lily is married and has three beautiful girls. Pamela is sick, though. She is still learning to walk at age 3. Kiki is also married with two kids and lives in Kigali.

Both Lily and Kiki graduated from college. I'm very proud of them. Valery also graduated from college a few years ago. He is very smart and has good career prospects.

Thierry graduated from high school. He is an auto mechanic. He did not like academics like the rest of us, but I think he will do fine. We will support him. He is very wise, kind, and smart. But sometimes I wonder whether the trauma of war does not still weigh on him. He was very young, and he did not deserve to witness horror. Not that anyone did. He seems to be doing fine though. He works for a tea factory in the South-West.

My father had a child with Vianney. His name is Gentil. He has brown skin—much lighter than the rest of us—but still has Dad's ears like all of us. He is studying architecture and should do well in life too. The first years after my father, Kiki, and Thierry returned from Congo were tough. Dad did not get back his teaching job right away, but he got a construction job. Thank God he is versatile. We had to destroy our beautiful, big house and move because of the "resettlement policy." But every time I dream of being home, I still see myself in our old home. I think Dad was devastated about being forced to demolish his own house without compensation. But in Rwanda everyone is treated like a soldier. You do not question a government policy. On a positive note, though, the house we moved into, on the main road, has electricity now. Dad plans to retire soon. He will not get a good retirement package, but we will help him some. He deserves a happy retirement.

I live in the United States now. I fled my country. I could not stand not being able to talk about the crimes I survived. It was too hard for me and I was afraid I might end up in prison or disappeared. I like it here. I have made lots of friends from every race and background. I am a global citizen now. I pray the political elite will forgive me and let me visit my country.

I miss my family and worry about them. I hope they won't pay for my stubbornness. I miss my country too. I love it so much and hope I can return at some point. I miss the village where I grew up. The green rolling hills of Zaza, and the dusty roads and playgrounds where I played soccer. I also miss the lit clean streets of Kigali that I strolled at night as I came home from dancing. I miss my friends, or bad goats as I call them. I miss going to French masses at Centre Christus.

I miss walking through chemin des amoureux, the tree-covered street between Petit Séminaire de Zaza and Lycée de Zaza. I miss walking through the banana plantations on the sunny days of the summer, and harvesting honey from banana flowers. I miss banana juice, and the ripe bananas from Grandma's kitchen. I miss the avocados and mangoes. The handball games in Groupe Scolaire de Zaza, and the DJs playing Kassav, Mukusa, and Boys II Men.

But mostly I miss and love you.

Petit

My Father

After the RPF came to power, I lived in constant fear that my father could go to prison at any time. Almost all the Hutu intellectuals from my district were detained on genocide allegations. Although my father never told us our ethnic affiliation, I knew he had been a member and a local leader of President Habyarimana's ruling party (MRND). But no one ever accused him of committing genocide. The only time anyone tried to smear him was during local elections when a certain man, for reasons I disregard, tried to tarnish his reputation by saying he did not qualify as a candidate because he had been a member of the MRND party. Many people overwhelmingly rallied behind my father, and I would later learn that the man was trying to get him jailed so he could illegally take over my father's eucalyptus forest behind the man's house. At that time, it was common for anyone with power to put people in jail and grab their property if they could link them somehow to the genocide.

Genocide survivors in my village seemed to be some of our

best family friends. Even the Tutsi who returned from Burundi interacted with us in a genuinely friendly way. I was very proud of my father and knew he was a man of high integrity who was respected by everyone in my town, and perhaps this was true because we'd always interacted kindly with people of all backgrounds. Nevertheless, I went through bouts of shame that my father had been a member of President Habyarimana's party. The idea that he had been a member of a major political party from a defeated regime that was accused of committing genocide was not something I was willing to accept about my family background. I did not want anyone to know that fact.

I would later learn that my father had refused to start a local chapter of the notorious Interahamwe—a youth branch of the ruling party, the militia that took the lead in murdering innocent Tutsi and moderate Hutu. This could have been the main reason why no one, not even for retribution purposes, pointed a finger at him even though he would have been an easy target. This was the period when, if a genocide survivor said you were involved in the genocide, you would immediately get detained without trial. Even when the Gacaca courts (the transitional justice courts) came, no one accused my father of anything.

In Rwanda, after the genocide, and even today to some degree, collective guilt rhetoric is normal. Many angry genocide survivors and Tutsis from various diasporas painted all Hutus with one broad brush, and shamed them without any consequence. It became normal to condone behavior or speech that placed blame for the genocide on all those who identified as Hutu. Some people use the term Interahamwe to refer to *all* Hutus, regardless of whether they had supported the genocide or opposed it, protected Tutsis, or lost their loved ones at the hands of genocide perpetrators. Being a Hutu meant walking with your eyes on the ground. Kids could be bullied on the basis that their fathers were detained for alleged genocide crimes, whether they were guilty or innocent.

Since my father was never accused or jailed even though he had been a member of the MRND, I did not face such bullying. In my early teenage years while attending the seminary, I started developing the capacity to understand the complexity of the tragedies that had befallen my country. My school focused on classical studies, encouraged critical thinking, and taught me to value the wisdom of philosophers like Aristotle and Socrates, as well as Saint Thomas of Aquinas. I used my philosophical studies to reflect on what my family had gone through, and I began to more clearly understand how my father had honorably tried to live by his principles during the horrors that befell our country and in their aftermath.

Making Sense of My Identity and Rwandan Inter-Ethnic Conflicts by Resisting Binary Thinking

Not infrequently, revolutionaries themselves become reactionary by falling into sectarianism in the process of responding to the sectarianism of the Right.

—Paulo Friere
Pedagogy of the Oppressed

My father's example of principled living would help me on my healing journey. I knew I had to forgive, to let go of resentment, anger, and hatred. But whom was I even resenting? I did not know the names of those who killed my grandfather and cousin; neither did I know the identity of those who might have killed my mother and sister Petite. The only thing I knew, and was sure of, was that the killers were affiliated with the Rwanda Patriotic Army. But the RPA, under the Rwanda Patriotic Front was in power. They were the victors of the war, the celebrated heroes who stopped the genocide and defeated the genocidal regime. Was the RPF as a whole also responsible for the deaths of my loved ones and for attempting to kill me on several occasions with my family? Was I supposed to hate them as an institution, and their leaders—my leaders—too? The president, cabinet, and parliament? Was I supposed to hate the whole leadership of the country? In other words, was I against the government? If not, who was responsible for the massacres I survived, and how was I supposed to relate to them? Was I going to find justice? What would justice look like for me?

I would not be able to name my attempted executioners, nor recognize them if I saw them today. I was just eight years old and I had never seen those men before. But I remember their uniforms. It was the same uniform that the military proudly continued to wear after 1994, and they had every right to be proud. They had won the war and put an end to a genocide. They had ended decades of oppression that many Rwandans endured and committed themselves to creating a government of unity in which all Rwandans would see themselves represented, not as Hutu, Tutsi, or Twa, but as Rwandans.

There was something to be proud of in the Mukotanyi uniform, and yet, it evoked traumatic memories for me. Every time I saw a soldier, I would remember the noise of gunfire as the Inkotanyi shot through our shelters on Kanazi hill, the morning I got separated from my family. Or, I would see the endless lines of RPA soldiers marching past my grandfather's house in Gatare going to murder those they believed were their unarmed enemies, their boots and the white sneakers that some of them wore making a scary rhythmic noise. And I would replay the scenes of my grandfather's and cousin's assassinations, which happened on that very day. I would remember my grandfather begging for our lives to be spared, my cousin crying as I ran zigzagging away, as the soldiers shot him multiple times in the back. And I would imagine the refugee camps being raided and my mother panicking and going separate ways from my father and two siblings, never to be seen again.

Somehow I was locked in a box with people who had endured the wrath of RPA soldiers avenging the genocide of Tutsi. But was I even Hutu? Tutsi? Twa? I could deduce from the fact that we were not targeted during the genocide that we were Hutu. I could make my own conclusions.

Or could I?

I recalled that my paternal uncle Rudoviko told my sister Lily that our family had identified as Tutsi historically, but that my grandfather managed to get Hutu identity cards when things started to get dangerous for Tutsis after the 1959 revolution. But I did not know what to believe, and I never bothered confirming the story with my father. In my village, my family was mostly known for our Abacyaba clan, which myth holds was founded by Nyirarucyaba, who is credited with bringing cows into the Kingdom of Rwanda. According to another legend, my ancestors migrated south from Ndorwa, the northeastern savanna area now home to the Akagera National Park, in search of pasture for their cows. I have not met anyone else from my clan outside my village, but I know clansmen felt a sense of pride about being Umucyaba. Despite this pride, I never felt any sense of belong-ingness to any clan or tribe or ethnicity, and my father never inculcated that in us as kids.

I was therefore always a bit confused when other people

would remark on who we looked like, or which ethnic group we belonged to. One middle-aged, tall teacher who'd returned from Burundi after the genocide called me "Mucyaba" every time he saw me, in reference to my clan. Our other neighbors who identified themselves as Tutsis, and who had lived in Burundi in exile for thirty years, reminded my sisters that we were Tutsi, that we did not look Hutu. They had assumed that we were Hutu from the mere fact that we had not survived the genocide against the Tutsi, but they were also confused because stereotypically, we had Tutsi features. They and others often reminded me that I was tall and had all the features of a Tutsi. Part of me liked that fact and wanted people to continue to consider me that way. I didn't have any problem with how I was physically built and how I looked. I was quite pleased that I was tall, and fitted the stereotypes of attractiveness in Rwanda as a tall, dark-skinned man. The concept of physical beauty was highly associated with being Tutsi. Very often people would say that Tutsis were beautiful and Hutus were not as attractive. But my soul wanted to recognize beauty in everyone. I wanted to be just human.

My siblings had similar experiences, especially in boarding schools, where people did not know everybody's background. Other students would assume our tuition was paid by the Genocide Survivor's Fund (FARG). Some of my sister's Tutsi friends would confess to her their resentment and hate toward Hutu children or warn her against hanging out with the Hutu students at school. I also realized that children who identified themselves as Tutsi tended to be more comfortable around me unlike those who, depending on what their experiences were during the genocide, could be said to be Hutu. Every time I chatted with friends who assumed I was Tutsi, our conversation was awkward. Our friendship was founded on the wrong reasons—or at least on reasons I did not believe should be the basis of any relationship. Inside, I felt that I was betraying my core principles, instilled in me by my father. I was betraying the bold and principled young man I knew myself to be. But at the same time, I did not fit into the identity binaries of my country—by nature, nurture, or principle. Would I ever be able to define my identity in a country where identity had been so politicized and polarized that it had caused a genocide?

My father had taught me to be authentic and honest. But he had also used the French word "sage" to invoke the Rwandan kind of wisdom which means "cautious." While this was not necessarily troublesome advice, it was rather awkward. I never knew whether I should correct someone's assumption that I was Tutsi, or not. They seemed so convinced that I was Tutsi, and that certainty seemed to serve them, and me, well.

"After all there was no evidence of differences between Hutu and Tutsis," I naïvely told myself. The two groups, as well as the Twa—whom we too often forget—shared the same culture and language. They lived as neighbors on the thousand hills of Rwanda for centuries. What "ethnic" identity was I supposed to choose? Or did I have the liberty to pick? I fought these labels, but they kept coming back right at me.

In the end, I decided I would tell those who were curious about my background that I was neither Tutsi nor Hutu. I chose to be considered just Rwandan and human. Of course, they would ask manifold follow-up questions, and many, including my girlfriend mentioned earlier, thought I was crazy for not having any ethnic affiliation, while others were very amused. But I persisted in summoning the courage to talk about ethnic identification in Rwanda, and most importantly to assert to my Tutsi friends that I was neither Tutsi nor Hutu. I started having fun with it. I was reminded too often that I was naïve, but I think naïve is the wrong word to describe my intentions. I was *bold. Radical. Stubborn*. And of course, *right*. I was determined to define my own identity based on *facts. Truth*. I believed that no one had the right to define who I was. It was my right to do that. I *strongly* believed that we were more than just products of heredity, environment, and history. We are spiritual beings living a physical reality, and we are not just one with all human beings, but with all beings. Our identities are more complex than we like to admit.

I would later realize that the reason I could not fit neatly into the Rwandan story was rooted in the limitations of simplistic, binary thinking. The polarization of the Rwandan conflict that culminated in a genocide was a result of this lazy, black-and-white way of understanding regarding people as Tutsi or Hutu, short or tall, dark-skinned or light-skinned. Put in mathematical terms, aggregates didn't tell the whole story, nor did simplistic, binary thinking. The Rwandan equation did not just have two unknowns. It was a multi-step equation with more than one variable, and with fractions and terms inside parentheses, which would take more thinking and more operations to solve. By over-simplifying the equation and trying to solve it with basic algebraic rules, we missed nuances of the story.

My personal identification as Rwando-human fits well with the official RPF's position. However, individuals, including RPF members, often still discriminate in private. The result can be stories told at kitchen tables and during private conversations that I want to bring out. I want to advocate for more open dialogue about identity, allowing Rwandans to share their stories. Some people might like to keep their "ethnic" identities. Others might want to reject them, like I do, but as long as we don't use identities to oppress and put down others, and as long as we embrace the Rwandan human identity above all other sub-identities, we will have peace.

Politicians, wittingly and sometimes unwittingly, exploited this binary thinking to achieve disastrous ends. I looked for stories of people in the gray areas of the Rwandan spectrum, and I could not find them. They were not told aloud, and yet they explained more about human nature and the causes of ethnic violence than the black-and-white political propaganda ever could. I knew these stories *had* to be told to solve the Rwandan puzzle, to ensure we learn a complete lesson from the costly tragedy that befell our country. If I could develop critical thinking and push back on this simplistic and flawed way of thinking that results in dividing people, breaking nations, and killing millions, maybe I could play a role in stopping further unnecessary bloody conflicts.

Your Heroes/My Villains?

All violence is the result of people tricking themselves into believing that their pain derives from other people and that consequently those people deserve to be punished.

—Marshall B. Rosenberg

The biggest challenge for reconciliation in Rwanda has been that the victory of the RPF and the liberation of the Tutsis was inevitably done through violence and war that unfortunately inflicted suffering on Hutus. As *The New York Times* columnist Maureen Dowd wrote in an opinion piece about celebrities who abuse children, "Celebrity supersedes criminality," and President Kagame and the RPF quickly became celebrities for stopping the genocide against the Tutsi and for rebuilding the country from the ashes of the conflict. Then, most Tutsis and the international community completely ignored the fact that the RPA (the

Inkotanyi), the rebel group that stopped the genocide and the national army it became, orchestrated killings against innocent civilians in both Rwanda and the Democratic Republic of Congo. How could the president be both a hero and a villain? After all, public opinion held that Kagame and his army could never be as cruel as the Interahamwe militia, so the lesser of the two evils was the hero, and the crimes some of his RPA soldiers committed were pushed under the rug.

I was pushed under the rug.

My mother and sister were pushed under the rug.

My cousin Kennedy was pushed under the rug.

My friend Blaise was pushed under the rug.

My grandfather and cousin were pushed under the rug.

Victims of these crimes were not commemorated in April, and no one would know they even existed.

I could not even pay homage to the victims publicly or tell their stories.

I remember always wishing my friends who survived the genocide against the Tutsi would—at least—tell me they regretted that the RPA killed my grandfather and cousin and tried to kill me, too. I remember wanting to tell them that I empathized with *their* suffering and wished they understood and acknowledged *my* suffering.

Beyond this personal wish, the debate about reconciliation in certain intellectual circles centers on the question of whether the Rwanda Patriotic Front can claim moral superiority, since some of them also killed innocent people, including women, children, and the elderly, just like the genocide perpetrators did. The RPA soldier heroes who rescued Tutsis from unimaginable carnage (sometimes finding their own relatives exterminated) committed crimes against humanity through retaliation or vengeance killings driven by anger, and by a collective-guilt mentality that many held against the Hutus. Hutus and other Rwandans who suffered violence perpetrated by the Rwanda Patriotic Army have not forgiven the RPA for those crimes that took the lives of their loved ones. Therefore, they get trapped into the binary thinking that supposes that if their suffering is not acknowledged and its perpetrators punished, they don't have an obligation to empathize with the victims of the genocide against the Tutsi.

This is the basis of what the RPF often refers to as "the double genocide ideology," or "genocide revisionism." Meanwhile, some Tutsi genocide survivors, and those who identify themselves as Tutsi, believe that Hutus who died during the liberation war deserved it, meaning that the RPA avenged them, since, after all, the conflict opposed Tutsis against Hutus. Though drawing any moral equivalence would be preposterous by any stretch of imag- ination, the situation is more complex than most people think. It has a political dimension. Those who identify themselves, or used to identify themselves, as Hutus are still the majority in Rwanda, and there is no evidence they have rid themselves of their resentment against the Rwanda Patriotic Front for the retaliation crimes committed against them.

I know a lot of people feel that the RPA/RPF should be legally held accountable for the crimes they committed, but I do not think this would necessarily be good for the country. Rwandans need to put the interests of the state before their own interests if they care to build a unified and prosperous nation. However, it is important that the RPA/RPF issue a public apology to those whose loved ones were killed by some of their members. They should condemn those crimes and allow the survivors to tell their stories and have an official commemoration day. Doing nothing, or trying to erase parts of history, hoping they can suppress the resentment of millions of Rwandans until they are dead and replaced by young people who do not share those grievances, is a mistake. Those who witnessed the crimes still have a long life to live, and they might be sharing those grievances with their children at kitchen tables.

A recognition of our common destiny is the only thing that is going to save the country, but for this realization to take place, people need to heal. Healing is not something that has been given the attention it deserves in Rwanda. A lot of people still live with post-traumatic stress disorder (PTSD), and most of them do not acknowledge it or know it. Churches, which are supposed to facilitate the healing given the deficit of trauma treatment, shy away from talking freely about these issues because of their political implications. For true national healing to take place, there must be a national truth and reconciliation program in which people can share their stories. Hutus must acknowledge the genocide against the Tutsi and utterly condemn it. They should refrain from conflating RPA war crimes with the genocide against the Tutsi. They should apologize if they, in any way, committed hate crimes or acts of genocide against Tutsis. Meanwhile, Tutsis should also acknowledge that all Hutus did not support the genocide, and they should be able to empathize with innocent civilians, mostly Hutus, whose loved ones perished at the hands of the RPA. They should understand that their heroes who saved them are not saints. They committed crimes they should not have committed against innocent countrymen. Two wrongs do not make a right.

Such a truth and reconciliation program can only take place if there is an internal debate in the RPF about how to handle the issue of "inter-ethnic" conflict because these grievances could spiral into another violent clash in the future. If people still see themselves as Hutus or Tutsis, chances are good that some politicians will exploit those identities and grievances for their political gains at some point in the future. After all, there is no guarantee that when Kagame is no longer president, his vision for national unity will be continued. Luckily, Rwanda has made a lot of progress to reduce "ethnic" discrimination in all spheres of life. However, nepotism is not something that one can completely control, and it is very likely that those with political power will continue to give favors to their relatives and friends, which could impose an "ethnic" dimension on political power.

The army is also another institution where Tutsis have a lot of influence given the fact that most leaders also participated in the liberation war. This is a problem that needs to be dealt with in the future since Rwandans still see each other through "ethnic" lenses—even if they are seldom vocal about it. Rwandans will need to be reassured that their government and other national institutions represent them and that they can see themselves in them.

If these issues are not resolved, Tutsis will likely maintain a tight grip on power since doing so would be the only way they could be guaranteed safety given the fact that they are a minority. But history shows that this is not a sustainable approach, since it engenders grievances of the silent majority. As much as I prefer the constitutional design of integration that does not guarantee quota representation for ethnic groups in the government, as in Burundi, the Rwandan leadership will need a lot of wisdom to ensure Rwandans do not suspect that one "ethnic" group holds more power than the other or gets more opportunities than the other. If for example, at some point, it starts to look like most rich people are Tutsi or Hutu, that could create grievances and revive old ethnic hatred.

The leadership will need to ensure justice and equal opportunity for Rwandans of all backgrounds without necessarily being loud about it. To put it differently, just like so-called colorblindness is ineffectual in healing racial divides in the United States, ethnic blindness will not solve the problem, especially if Rwandans can find out who's Hutu or Tutsi. If a certain ethnic group is predominant in any Rwandan institution, people will notice, and the perceived inequity could breed strife. The government must institute all possible measures to deal with the loopholes that could be used by some people to maintain "group" supremacy, and it must be intentional about doing so. It is going to be important that patterns of supremacy of one social group of Rwandans do not appear structural in any way, no matter how haphazard they might be in nature.

Wrestling with Truth

When you wrestle with your consciousness and lose,
you actually win.

—Unknown

Only my personal healing could lead me to the point where I was able to see the need for healing on a national level. Growing up in Rwanda, I saw myself as a victim. "After all, I was only eight years old," I often told myself. I did not understand what was going on, nor did I know my ethnicity. Obviously, I was an innocent victim, right? Which made those who tried to kill me and who had killed my grandfather and cousin, guilty perpetrators. By every meaning, I was innocent.

But was I?

My childish thinking told me that if these people had tried to kill me and my family, something must have been wrong with us, with me. The judge in my mind taunted me with guilty thoughts, especially as I grew up and realized that my would-be assassins were associated with the military leadership of the country—the heroes who had stopped the genocide. If I had survived crimes committed by the lauded victors, I must have been a bad person. Feelings of guilt and shame mixed with those of victimhood and sadness ate at me. I did not know how to feel, nor how to heal.

As I've recounted, most of the rhetoric I heard did not seem to sympathize with me. None of the stories I heard at commemoration events alluded to the crimes I survived. But I still went to commemorate with all Rwandans—after all, the victims of the genocide against Tutsis looked like me, and most of them considered me one of theirs. They were my family, friends, and compatriots.

As I healed, I not only understood that I was innocent, but also that my family had been against the genocide. It was a relief to know, and it soothed my guilt and shame, though not entirely. My assailants did not know my family, and even if they had perceived my family as being on the wrong side of history, under no circumstances did I deserve their vengeance. I would later understand that the conflict was polarized to the extent that anyone some RPA soldiers suspected was Hutu was assumed to deserve death, including children and the elderly, in many instances.

As I got older, I started to understand better the scope and context of the crimes I survived. The British Broadcasting Corporation (BBC) aired shows debating the issue of people who were killed by the RPA. The official response from the RPF leadership was that some soldiers had carried out revenge killings as they arrived in what used to be their villages to save their families, only to find that their families had been exterminated, and they could not contain their urge to kill those whom they suspected were responsible for the murders of their family members. But the truth was that multiple systematic killings of men, women, the elderly, and children had been carried out across the country.

As for my mother, I understood that the refugee camps in which she stayed with my father and two siblings harbored militiamen who were responsible for the genocide and who were reorganizing to attack Rwanda. I understood the need for Rwanda to repatriate refugees and prevent the genocidal machine and Interahamwe militias from reorganizing, recruiting refugees, and attacking Rwanda again. But did destroying the camps mean killing innocent children and mothers? Could they not distinguish civilians from armed militia and EX-FAR?

"Maybe it was not easy. I am not a military strategist," I phlegmatically thought.

Then reports came out, including the UN report mapping human rights violations by different players in the First Congo War, and it turned out that the Rwandan Army had carried out mass killings of unarmed refugees.

The reality became more and more complicated for me to bear. What I was learning pointed to the fact that the conflict in Rwanda was polarized to the point where Hutu extremists killed Tutsis indiscriminately, and it looked like the RPA/RPF and the Rwanda Defense Force (RDF), occasionally, had also indiscriminately killed those they deemed to be Hutus, including children and the elderly—as was the case for my grandfather and cousin. Whether these soldiers had received orders from above remained unknown. But judging by the scope of the killings, it became clear to me that some military leaders might have ordered, or at least overlooked, the killings.

For the twenty-one years I spent in Rwanda after the

genocide, I did not hear of anyone being prosecuted for crimes committed by the RPF/RPA. Some RPA top leaders did mention that some soldiers were prosecuted in military courts, but I never heard about their trials, nor did I hear a simple acknowledgement or apology.

Then came international arrest warrants from French and Spanish judges against top RPF leaders, including President Kagame, which sparked a diplomatic crisis between Rwanda and France. Part of me was content that at least someone knew about these crimes and wanted to do something about them. But then I thought, as objectively as I could, had they arrested RPF military leaders and prosecuted them, would this have meant justice to me? Were France's intentions just? I must admit that at some point, I thought so.

I would later come to the realization that prosecuting top RPF military leaders would not bring me justice, and that France's intentions were political and geopolitical. So, what did justice mean anyway?

Justice

Common sense suggested that those responsible for my suffering had to endure some form of punishment for me to find justice. Every time I heard news that courts were trying to bring RPF leaders before justice—including President Kagame, who had been the leader of the RPF military wing, RPA—I felt the urge to support the idea. I looked forward to the day they would be brought to account for the crimes they had committed, and at some point, I felt that my mission would be to do whatever I could to make sure they paid for their actions.

But with time, I understood that if the leaders of the RPF did face justice in a court of law, the country would likely descend into chaos. Though I continued to be bothered by the fact that top RPF leaders were still unapologetic for the crimes they had committed, I also realized that sending them to The Hague would not mean justice for me. For the sake of the country, I understood that justice as we defined it under the law would not necessarily be the answer to healing the nation, let alone healing myself.

The only question that remained unanswered for me was whether they didn't want to admit these crimes and apologize because their legitimacy would be undermined and Hutu radicals emboldened, or whether they didn't want to apologize because they felt they were justified in killing innocent Rwandans. To me, the latter possibility indicated a true heartlessness that could only be detrimental to the unity of the country. For the sake of the country's unity and future, I didn't wish to see RPF leaders behind bars, but I thought this was a question that required an answer if the country was going to heal the wounds of disunity and move on.

In my lengthy, painful, cathartic reflections on the atrocities I had survived, and on the lack of remorse on the part of the people who were indirectly or directly associated with them, I came to the realization that the best form of justice would be the one that would heal my pain. I came to understand that I had to reclaim my power to give justice to myself, and I learned that this power lies in forgiveness. I progressed in my thinking toward the idea that it's okay to lose an enemy, and I took inspiration from the following words of Dr. Martin Luther King, Jr.:

> *We must develop and maintain the capacity to forgive.*
> *He who is devoid of the power to forgive is devoid of the*
> *power to love. There is some good in the worst of us and*
> *some evil in the best of us. When we discover this,*
> *we are less prone to hate our enemies.*

Forgiveness was a remedy prescribed by many other spiritual and intellectual luminaries, too, and the ingredients of this healing potion were truth, empathy, and self-love. I embarked on a journey to love myself unconditionally and heal the unjustified guilt and shame I had felt—that somehow I deserved to

witness the death of my grandfather and become motherless—
and pursued these pillars of forgiveness, self-love, empathy, and
truth *as* justice.

My pursuit was grounded in the conviction that there was
nothing wrong with me or my family. After all, those who had
attempted to take my life did not know me. Though I could
guess the reason for their ignominious acts, I could not tell with
certainty the motive of their actions.

I know now that there was nothing personal about the fact
that these people tried to kill me and my family. I had nothing
to do with the conflict, and neither did my family. I did not identify myself as Hutu, nor did I understand what that identity
entailed.

I was not Tutsi either—even if my friends and I, too often,
wanted me to be Tutsi. I did not have to fit into the binaries
that conflict entrepreneurs had created or hardened to maintain
themselves in power. I did not have to perpetuate centuries of
division and oppression. I did not have to hate anybody.

I knew that if I wanted to heal, I would have to love those
who, on multiple occasions, had attempted to take my life, and
who had taken the lives of my grandfather, cousin, mother, and
sister. I would have to love those whom I knew and didn't know,
those who still believed that my family and I deserved to die.
But I could not love them without forgiving them. I also had to
forgive myself for wishing them bad, and I had to stop being so
hard on myself.

My good judgement told me that if I judged others, I had to
look at my own dirty laundry. I knew I loved and empathized
with the victims of the genocide against the Tutsis. They were
the victims. Their bitterness towards those responsible for their
plight was natural. I was also aware that many of them tended

to broaden the blame to all those who identified as Hutus, and I completely understood why they would do that. Not many Hutus had been bold enough to protect their Tutsi neighbors. Many had been bystanders, and others had passively supported their demise. How could I blame the Tutsi for assuming these things of the Hutus? I knew humanity's tribal-thinking brain can trick us into categorizing and generalizing, especially when we perceive or experience danger. I chose to empathize with the Tutsis even if I knew most of them did not empathize with those who had survived war crimes committed by their saviors. I knew the consciousness this thinking required, and the healing it took to get there was not readily accessible by many people in Rwanda—at least not at the same time as I accessed it.

I had to transcend basic instinctual impulses and hold myself to a much higher standard if I truly wanted to be a peacemaker. If I criticized others for not learning enough from the genocide, I had to hold myself to a higher consciousness: to empathize with those who did not empathize with me. It was not politically correct—in fact it was fatal—to ask for empathy for the war crimes I had survived at the hands of the RPA, so I endeavored to learn to understand those who did not even try to understand me, whether genuinely or pragmatically. I knew hate and negative emotions were not an option for me if I wanted to truly heal, so loving those who did not wish me well was the only option left.

I evolved to believe that what had happened to me, while tragic, was not unfair or unjust. I realized that every time I saw the world and my experiences through the eyes of injustice, I would have to find someone to blame and seek justice. I understood, mostly thanks to Baha'i writings, that I was organic with the world around me, with the universe, and that when a tragedy of this magnitude strikes, no one should expect to remain unaffected. I reclaimed the power to decide how to react and interpret the traumatic experiences I had gone through. I stopped taking the murders I had survived *personally*. I was not a bad person. I was not the villain in the story.

Yes, justice for me was *forgiveness*. Forgiving *myself* and freeing myself from resentment towards those who did not sympathize with my suffering. My healing and happiness *only* depended on *me*. I did not need approval, sympathy, apology, or justice from anyone else but *myself*. Those who had committed crimes against my family and me had debased themselves. They were the ones with a problem. Not me. I chose to forgive them, not because they deserved it, but because I deserved to heal and to be happy. I did not want them to have power over me. To control my happiness.

I still thought that those representing my offenders had to make a public apology for the sake of unifying and healing the country. I understood that they feared losing legitimacy, and emboldening the opposition—their political enemies. They thought like politicians. But at the same time, I worried that if they did not regret the crimes they were responsible for, they were doing a disservice to the country, and inflicting great damage to its unity. I worried that so many people had not forgiven them, which might result in strife in the future. I did not know if they had also healed, or whether they had reconciled. I constantly asked myself whether we (Rwandans) had learned from the genocide, and what my role could be in bringing more healing, peace, and unity to my country.

I was not in control of many factors but I could tell the truth of what happened—impartially. I had heard different accounts of the genocide and war, but many people tended to get caught up in the blame game instead of taking responsibility. I was a child during the genocide and war, and I did not commit any crime, but I felt the responsibility to tell the truth and help my countrymen heal and move on.

Cultivating Our Gardens:
Victimhood vs. Responsibility

Some are guilty but all are responsible.
—Abraham Joshua Heschel

If there's anything I learned from witnessing the horrors of the genocide and attempting to understand what had happened to my people, it is that people want only to believe themselves to be nice and well-intentioned. A belief in good and evil as external forces absolves us of responsibility, which we like, because we can then avoid the fact that evil is part of us (or rather that if we understand evil as the absence of goodness, we all fall short of goodness very often). We like to protect ourselves from guilt and shame, and understandably so—they are not fun feelings.

I witnessed and survived unimaginable suffering because the conflict in Rwanda was polarized when people were not courageous enough to seize the goodness within themselves and stand up to the radicals who appealed to the basest nature of humans and descended us all into the abyss. Everyone was guilty. I reckoned that if good people failed to take risks to prevent innocent people from being murdered, they were also responsible— not responsible in the sense that they deserved to be murdered in revenge, but responsible for inaction nevertheless. I was eight years old and caught up in this polarized, self-destructing fratricide just because adults failed to reconcile their differences and stop themselves from unleashing hell upon our country. They were caught up in a frenzy, refusing to recognize humanity in fellow human beings.

And as the RPA fought the monsters, some of its members became like the monsters they were fighting. They gazed into the abyss, and the abyss stared back at them, and I was caught up between the two monsters. To me, every Rwandan was responsible; even not speaking out constituted culpability. Whether Hutus who stood by as Tutsis were being hacked like banana trees, or Tutsis who watched some members of the Rwanda Patriotic Army carry out killings against innocent civilians and took it as bringing justice to their deceased families.

After the genocide and war, many who narrated stories of what happened, whether victims or perpetrators, referred to some external force as a factor. Often, people said Satan had taken over the country, or that people were possessed by demons. Rwandans who believed the myth that God slept in their country wondered where He had slept during those 100 days. Mourning songs asked where God had been. "Mana waruri he?" (Where were you, God?) became the recurring question.

No one seemed to take responsibility.

People who murdered children did not give any explanation

as to why they committed such unimaginable acts of violence against harmless beings.

It added to my frustration that the religion that failed to prevent people from killing seemed to grant them reasons to avoid responsibility by blaming Satan, or citing the absence of God. Those same people also believed that God was omnipresent, omniscient, omnipotent, merciful, and loving. God was their savior and King, and He embodied all the good attributes. This sounded contradictory, and I did not tolerate contradiction and confusion.

Growing up in a religious family, the concept of God was inculcated in me at a very young age. Even when my grandfather was told to lie on his belly and face his fate, I was reciting "Hail Mary" and "Our Father." As I jumped and ran, I was still praying.

For a long time, I wanted to believe that I survived because I prayed, but it did not seem convincing to me, since automatically I had to wonder whether my grandfather died because he did not pray, or my three-year-old cousin died because she did not know how to pray. What about my mother, my youngest sister, Kennedy, Abimana? What about the hundreds of thousands of other people who died?

I could not find proper answers to these questions. I later stumbled upon this quotation from Abraham Joshua Heschel: "Some are guilty but all are responsible." These words helped me to understand that even if the Rwanda Patriotic Army did not have any excuse to kill innocent people in revenge attacks, when something like a genocide occurs, people turn into ruthless beasts, and innocent people get hurt, including children.

This paradigm shift reminded me of my responsibility as a member of the human species to care about the suffering of other human beings, whoever and wherever they might be. In turn, it allowed me to grapple with a question that haunted me in the years after the genocide: Why did I survive?

Was it pure coincidence? In the Rwandan philosophy, when somebody dies, people believe that God has called them to be with Him. The idiom that people widely use when somebody dies is "Kwitaba Imana," which translates to "responding to God's call." Though it might sound like euphemism to non-Rwandans, it is a belief held by a majority of Rwandans, and it predates Christianity and Islam. But this long-held thinking did not make sense to me because the victims of genocide and war did not die natural deaths.

Or, is there any such thing as a natural death?

I wondered, if God could save lives of people and did not come to their rescue, did He love them?

Some people would even say that God loved the dead more than we did, so He/She/It took them to be with Him. Should we mourn their loss, then?

And did this mean that God did not love me and all the people who survived?

Did God love some people more than He loved others?

All these were questions that unceasingly lingered in my head.

But the most bothersome question of all was that of Satan. If God is believed to be more powerful, why did He let Himself be overpowered by Satan?

Or, maybe He did not care.

Though I still believed in God or the higher force, or an energy that is the only uncaused cause of all that is, I could not tell for sure whether God ever intervened in our lives—at least I knew God did not intervene in conflicts to save lives of innocent lives. Did this make God a passive force, or a neutral force that required our invitation to intervene in our lives? Whatever the answers to these questions, I believe that people ought to take responsibility for their actions and leave God out of their justifications.

In the end, I understood that God made His/Her/Its will and purpose known to us. He/She/It gave us spiritual laws like love, unity, and forgiveness. We have the free will to obey them or break them, and when we ignore them, we suffer, and innocent people suffer, as well.

This understanding was the only way I could keep God in the equation of life, tragedy, and death without raising contradictions in my mind. I could believe in God, and still accept the inevitability of death and tragedy. If God intervened in our lives, it wasn't to stop physical death. People must stop death and destruction. If God intervenes, it is *through* people with the moral courage to risk their lives to save other lives.

Death

Death is not the greatest loss in life.
The greatest loss is what dies inside us while we live.

—Norman Cousins

The fear of death follows from the fear of life.
A man who lives fully is prepared to die at any time.

—Mark Twain

Facing death as a child removed the illusion of my immortality and made me appreciate the gift of life. Knowing that I could die at any time made me choose to live my life to the fullest, and to lead a life free of moral debts towards others. But perhaps the most important lesson death taught me was to be courageous and to fight for truth and justice. It gave me the strength to be prepared for the worst, and to be happy *anyway*.

I figured that since I had survived, why choose to live an unhappy, unexamined, unfulfilled life? Life for me was not just breathing and having a healthy body, but living with a purpose.

I embraced my power and responsibility to *produce* emotions. I decided that now that I was in *charge*, why not produce *healthy, positive* emotions. I strongly believed that was what my mother and all my loved ones who passed away wanted me to do—that their passing should not leave me in a miserable state of mind.

I rewired my belief system and corrected all the beliefs that made me unhappy. I *unlearned* that our deceased loved ones somehow want us to be sad that they are gone to validate their importance in our lives. Instead, I strongly believed that they want us to be happy. That is how I decided to honor them.

I also *unlearned* that our dear departed ones want us to hate those who were responsible for their death. I *learned* that they did not want us to avenge them. I embraced the *power* I had within me to set a new belief system that did not lead me to suffering, and my country to unceasing self-destruction.

At first, I did not want to accept the reality that death is very much part of life. "I was young, and I deserved to live," I told myself. But the truth was that other people even younger than I, had perished. My three-year-old cousin was killed. Did I deserve to live more than she did?

I believed that death was a punishment. Yet, the truth is that we die every day as we change and grow older. Getting old is dying slowly. "But this is the natural death," I thought to myself. If death was natural, why did I not want to accept it? Like Khalil Gibran said, "For life and death are one, even as the river and the sea are one."

I came to the realization that I was not the one to choose who should live and who should die. Furthermore, the idea that there was a Higher Being who picked and chose who should die and who should live was absurd to me. By trying to justify why I had survived, I overrated my worth over those who had died. By thanking God that I had survived, it meant that I was somehow more fortunate than those who had died. Human mortality was baked in the randomness of the universe, so if I wanted to be happy, I had to accept the *truth* of life and death.

One of my favorite verses from Jesus was John 8:32, "...and you will know the truth, and the truth will set you free." I truly believed that he meant the naked, empirical truth of life. I did not want to live a life of illusions and fantasies. I wanted to face the reality of life head-on. The truth is that when tragedies hit, whether natural or man-made, even children get hurt.

I knew that my survival wasn't because I was any better or any more deserving of life. Therefore, dying or living were both the same. I realized that until I accepted death as an integral part of life, not two separate realties but one, I could not achieve peace and happiness. If I was going to live happily, I would have to learn not to fear death.

Just as an insecure lover can't be happy with their partner if they are always afraid of losing them, I would not be happy with my life until I was comfortable with the inescapable reality that I could lose it anytime. I learned from coming face to face with death as a young child, that loving people truly was knowing that they could disappear from one's life anytime. Psychologists speak of attachment issues for children who have been abandoned at a young age. I experienced it differently. Because I know that people are mortal and impermanent, I choose to enjoy their presence while I still can see them. But at the same time, I learned not to condition my happiness on their presence in my life.

Why had I not been taught that becoming an orphan was not something to be ashamed of? As much as we should love children who have lost their parents, it is as important to help them understand that death is a part of life, no one is in control of who lives and who dies, and that to be orphaned is not a sign of essential misfortune. Orphans should not feel like they are not whole, or like they are somehow lesser than children with both parents. I was a normal child just like those who had their mothers still living with them and nurturing them.

I've never understood why death was taboo and why I had not been taught that people die and that this is part of life. I have never understood why we (human beings) have not made peace with death, even if it is as old as life. Even if we kill all the time. We continue to see death as a punishment, even natural death. In fact, we are afraid of death to the extent that we are more likely to attend a funeral than a wedding.

We are afraid of dead bodies, and some cultures even have rituals to appease the spirits of the dead. Death has become a business for some religions to instill fear and guarantee life after death, conditional on certain behaviors determined righteous. Dictators use death to terrorize and oppress. Terrorists use it to paralyze the whole world. It only takes a few suicide attacks to cause panic in the entire world and make us abandon our moral obligations. Conflict entrepreneurs use fear of death to turn people into killing machines under the pretext of self-defense. Fear and insecurity have become good business for politicians and warmongers.

I realized that if I wanted to work for peace, I would have to deal with my fear of death. I came to understand that if everyone's main concern was to preserve their own life and they lacked the courage to die for justice and peace, the disciples of the Machiavellis of our time would continue to inflict pain on others, since they are aware that not enough people will rise and challenge them. I understood that the genocide did not happen because bad people outnumbered good people, but because "good" people stood by and watched. The impulse to preserve their lives at the expense of the justice of their neighbors was greater than their courage to save them. If I wanted to correct the thinking that keeps propagating destruction, I would have to be fearless. *Bold*.

Embracing the mortality of my physical life would save my life as it gave me purpose.

Happiness and Meaning

He who has a why to live can bear almost any how.
—Frederich Nietzsche

What would give me a sense of meaning and purpose after going through tragedy? Family? Belongingness? School? Sports? Money? I did not find answers to these questions right away. In fact, life went on in survival mode and I barely had time to pause and think about my condition. All I knew was that the world around me did not make sense, and I always asked questions. It wasn't until I shared my story in public, and people started asking me how I could live a normal life after what I had been through that I retroactively started to do an inventory of my past and present, or my "space-time," as Einstein might have called it.

Like many of my friends, I was determined to study hard, find a job, make money, and be happy in that linear order. Then I read a quote somewhere that said, "In your pursuit of happiness, remember to pause and be happy." That was the beginning of a long path to find what gave me a sense of meaning and happiness. I was quite a stoic, and still am, but since my encounter with this quote, I started embracing some epicureanism and giving myself permission to enjoy myself a little, to treat myself, and to then continue the endless pursuit of happiness. I realized that if I put conditions on happiness, I would never be truly happy, so I decided to be just happy, happy for no reason.

Death, sickness, orphanage, and unmet material needs were normal, so after losing my mother and staring at death in the face multiple times, I resolved not to let anything cause me anxiety anymore.

But all this was a process. I would never be too hard on myself when I felt anxious or sad. I would take time to meditate and just watch my thoughts like clouds moving through the sky, strive not to judge them, but to understand why those thoughts caused certain emotions in me. Through this process I would discover that my interpretation of the experiences I had been through or that occurred around me was the key determinant of the emotions I felt, so I chose to focus on my interpretation of how I experienced the world, which was mainly shaped by my *beliefs*. I grew to believe that thoughts that triggered strong emotions gave us clues about a reservoir of energy we needed to tap into—the source of our fire and passion. My job was to transform that energy into something positive, my motivation and purpose, the reason to wake up every morning and labor at something I valued.

I shared my thoughts with a fifteen-year-old Cameroonian immigrant teenager I was mentoring in the Jackson Square neighborhood of Boston. I was amazed to learn that he knew the concept and had an acronym for it, ETICA: Experience, Thought, Interpretation, Choice, and Action. I understood, from psychologists and neuroscientists that I followed online, that only self-awareness and interpreting the world in a mentally healthy way could improve my mental and physiological well-being. I found wisdom in other quotes I happened upon, like "Unless you learn to face your shadows, you will continue to see them in others, because the world outside you is only a reflection of the world inside you," and I determined to create for myself the reality I wanted for myself and for the world around me.

Understanding what happened to me as a young boy, how and why it had happened, and what I had to do to heal, while also thinking about how to prevent what happened to me and my country from ever happening again in the future, gave me purpose. *A reason to live.* The key, for me, was to find a way to bring clarity to the amalgam of emotions and thoughts caused by the trauma I had experienced. I found my purpose by diving into my past and finding where it hurt.

On the 22nd commemoration of the genocide, in 2016, I decided to share my personal journey of healing, understanding the causes of violence, and finding peace in a talk I gave at the University of Maine, at Orono, where I was pursuing my graduate studies. As I researched other people who had coped with tragedy, I stumbled upon a quote by Viktor Emil Frankl, an Austrian Jewish neurologist, psychiatrist, and Holocaust survivor, who said:

> What a man needs is not a tensionless state but rather the striving and struggling for some goal worthy of him. What he needs is not the discharge of tension at any cost, but the call of a potential meaning waiting to be fulfilled by him, hence the saying, meaningfulness, and not

happiness, is more important.

After my presentation one of my professors who was in the audience asked me, "How do you find meaning?"

I do not think that people get a sense of meaning from the same things, but everyone can find meaning, something to live for if they want. For some it could be family, others a talent to develop and use, and so on. Victor Frankl found the strength to fight to stay alive and not lose hope because of the love he had for his wife. Later when I encountered the Baha'i Faith, I came to the realization that meaning comes from selfless service to humanity.

As for the pursuit of happiness and success, Viktor Frankl gave the following advice, which I have strived to follow:

> Again and again I therefore admonish my students in Europe and America: Don't aim at success—the more you aim at it and make it a target, the more you are going to miss it. For success, like happiness, cannot be pursued; it must ensue. And it only does so as the unintended side effect of one's personal dedication to a cause greater than oneself or as the byproduct of one's surrender to a person other than oneself. Happiness must happen, and the same holds for success: you have to let it happen by not caring about it. I want you to listen to what your conscience commands you to do and go on to carry it out to the best of your knowledge. Then you will live to see that in the long-run, in the long-run, I say! success will follow you precisely because you had forgotten to think about it.

Another thinker whose insights resonated with me as I treaded the path to meaningfulness and happiness is Parker Palmer, an author, educator, and activist. In one of his speeches he said:

> Do not let heartbreaks break your hearts, but instead let them break your hearts open. Let suffering make you more compassionate, give you more capacity of heart to take in other people's sorrows and joys. Every day exercise your heart by taking in life's pains and joys. That kind exercise will make your heart supple the way a runner makes a muscle supple, so that when it breaks, (and it surely will,) it will break not into a fragment grenade, but into a greater capacity for love.

As I reflected on, and researched the theme of meaningfulness and happiness, love kept resurfacing as if a thread that bound everything about happiness together. My search consisted mostly of staying with the questions longer and waiting for answers to manifest. By doing that, I strangely kept attracting literature that explored this topic. Some of the spiritual writers whose works provided me with insights that helped me grow and heal into a more loving adult were Paul Ferrini, with his exploration of unconditional love, and Don Miguel Ruiz, with his work on the mastery of love and the agreements we make with ourselves. It was thanks to the works of these two authors that I realized that love was not a finite resource to be begged from other people, but an abundant source that anybody could tap into *within* themselves.

Don Miguel Ruiz's idea of the magical kitchen of love where anyone can cook the love recipe was quite liberating. I stopped looking for love outside of me, and instead rediscovered the inexhaustible source of love *within* me. But by far the most lifesaving epiphany was learning from Don Miguel Ruiz's *Mastery of Love*, that happiness does not come from receiving but from *giving*. To paraphrase his central ideas: Happiness and meaning come from giving love to oneself and others, forgiving oneself and others, and being truthful with oneself and others.

Truth, love, and forgiveness became my pillars of happiness and meaningfulness. I stopped expecting love, truth, and forgiveness *from* other people and chose to always *give* them to myself and others. For the first time, my happiness and meaningfulness did not depend on anyone or anything external to me, but were entirely dependent on me. Reclaiming my power and fully embracing my responsibility to live a happy and meaningful life was a turning point in my adult life.

Obedience to Authority, Group Pressure, and Conformity

It may be that we are puppets—puppets controlled by the strings of society. But at least we are puppets with perception, with awareness. And perhaps our awareness is the first step to our liberation.

—Stanley Milgram

My constant questions in the aftermath of the genocide have always been: How could this have happened? Were these people sadistic by nature? How could they have carried out such ignoble acts? But the most important of all the questions was: Have we learned from history? Or rather, what have we learned about human nature? And how can we educate people to make bolder and more humane decisions?

What was terrifying to me was that deep inside, I felt that how the aftermath was being managed was not addressing the core questions, hence not providing holistic solutions. I lived with constant fear that what happened could occur again.

Obedience, group pressure, and conformity made normal

people kill others because the authority and the majority deemed it heroic. Today, obedience and conformity are being used to consolidate power and ensure stability in a country where the leadership is made up of predominantly Tutsis who stopped the genocide, and those who survived it. Meanwhile, most of the citizenry is composed of Hutus who are still struggling with shame and guilt of finding themselves on the wrong and losing side of the conflict, but who also have legitimate grievances against the military wing of the current ruling party.

To be fair, after a genocide and a war, the first step of recovery is stabilization, and that requires ability to project power and influence throughout the country, and a strong central government. But also, in the case of Rwanda, stabilization means nation-building, since before the genocide different factions of the citizenry were not united and many had spent decades in exile.

Nation-building has also often required a common unifying narrative, and propaganda has been used to teach that narrative. Sadly, nation-state narratives have also often left out uncomfortable truths, like the extermination of Native Americans in the United States. The question is whether Rwanda can build a narrative that includes war crimes committed by the victors and liberators of the country. The Rwanda Patriotic Front's propaganda educates younger generations to embrace a national identity (which is laudable), but it has also constructed a Hollywood-like romantic narrative of the liberation war in which the RPA is an army of elite archangels who rescued Tutsi survivors with zero collateral damage. The problem with romanticizing the liberation war is that one implicitly puts collective guilt on all Hutus while minimizing and showing no sympathy or remorse for the killings many of them survived. It implies that babies, children, mothers, the elderly, and any other victims who died at the hands of the RPA soldiers were part of "adui," as they called the "enemy." This is dangerously problematic since most Hutus (especially not children and babies) did not commit the genocide, and it would be even hard to prove that they silently thought their innocent un-armed Tutsi neighbors should be lumped together with the then rebels (Rwanda Patriotic Army/Front) whom their government's propaganda trumpeted were coming to kill Hutus and subjugate them to their pre-colonial second-class citizenship.

The truth is that the "revenge" killings many soldiers of the Rwanda Patriotic Army carried out were reprehensible even by precolonial standards. The precolonial army, when it invaded a neighboring kingdom, killed most men since every man was considered a soldier then (and castrated them to bring proof they had killed the enemy, and used the testicles to adorn Karinga, the royal drum, symbol of the Rwandan Kingdom—you think Vikings were brutal?) but they did not kill women and children. My worry then, is that a substantial percentage of Rwandans today (even if the census doesn't collect data on survivors and victims of war crimes committed by the RPA) have survived or have relatives who have survived these crimes. How does the current ruling party then govern these people? How is it able to build legitimacy? How does a perceived minority class (which is responsible for war crimes by association or omission) rule over a majority that is responsible for a genocide against the minority (by association or omission)?

Everyone is supposed to be a member of the RPF—especially those in position of power and influence, including national and local elite from primary school teachers and local shop owners to government technocrats, and even popular artists. By making sure that everyone is inside the system, the RPF is able to limit dissent. There is no life outside of the party. Even students as young as high school age are sworn into the RPF (part of the oath says: "If I betray the party, I should be treated like any other enemy"). In fact, they argue that the RPF is not a party but the "family" of Rwandans, hence being an RPF member is synonymous with being a Rwandan. Free-thinking is discouraged and conformism celebrated. There are of course positive aspects of this model, though I reject how consensus is reached within the party, especially on the question of what to do about the war crimes committed by some members of the Rwanda Patriotic Army.

Though I might sound critical of the government, I am actually sympathetic. Rwanda is not an easy country to govern, especially not after the genocide and war, but I genuinely fear that lack of critical thinking and blind obedience could give people excuses to hurt others if their leader orders them to do so in the future—if it is not happening already. I worry that Rwandans might not have learned the important lessons from the genocide and war, an abysmal notion, since the price was more than a million precious lives (if you count Hutus who died, and soldiers from both sides of the war). I would like to believe that President Kagame and the ruling party have a plan to help the country continue to heal, and, at some point, address grievances of survivors of war crimes committed both in Rwanda and the Democratic Republic of Congo.

Breaking the Cycle of Violence: The Politics of Unity and Reconciliation

I realized that there was no end to making even.

—Unknown

One of my favorite writers, Paulo Freire, says in *Pedagogy of the Oppressed*:

> It is only the oppressed who, by freeing themselves, can free their oppressors. The latter, as an oppressive class, can free neither others nor themselves. It is therefore essential that the oppressed wage the struggle to resolve the contradiction in which they are caught; and the contradiction will be resolved by the appearance of the new man: neither oppressor nor oppressed, but man in the process of liberation. If the goal of the oppressed is to become fully human, they will not achieve their goal by merely reversing the terms of the contradiction, by simply changing poles.

Unlike South Africa, Rwanda's unity and reconciliation left out the Truth element. And this was not haphazard, for the truth would mean the whole truth: that there was a genocide against the Tutsis, and war crimes committed by the Rwanda Patriotic Army against innocent civilians.

In Rwanda, even the survivors of the genocide against the Tutsis don't always have the right to tell their truth, or have an opinion on policies of unity and reconciliation. When I worked with Never Again Rwanda, we took a group of participants in the Peace Building Institute to the Commission of Unity and Reconciliation, as they wished to learn what Rwanda could teach the world. It was at the beginning of the Ndi Umunyarwanda campaign, an initiative that was launched with a self-proclaimed Hutu artist who encouraged all Hutus to apologize for the genocide that was committed against Tutsis in their name.

At that time, the president of Ibuka, the association of survivors of the genocide against Tutsis, came out opposing the initiative, saying that individuals who were responsible for the genocide should ask for forgiveness in their own name to those they had offended.

One participant in the Peace Building Institute asked the deputy head of the then Unity and Reconciliation Commission what he thought about Ibuka's stance on Ndi Umuryarwanda, to which he replied, "The commission does not have an official position on the issue yet. I will let you know once we do."

In the following days, the representatives of genocide survivors were convoked at Centre Kabusunzu and told they had to support the campaign because President Kagame had publicly come out in support of the campaign saying, "If someone commits a crime in my name and does not apologize for it, I would kill him myself."

As mentioned earlier, a year later, Kizito Mihigo, a music composer and singer, then a darling of the office of the president, and a survivor of the genocide against Tutsis himself, possibly inspired by his Catholic faith or political dissidents opposed to the Kigali regime, composed the song he called "The Meaning of Death" in which he recognized the pain of those who survived crimes "that were not called genocide" but that happened within the same period of 100 days. He suddenly disappeared, and his song was never played on any radio station-public and private. Whether it was censored by the government or whether the media censored itself, remains a mystery. He was later accused of plotting with the opposition to overthrow the government. All his other songs had been widely played during the genocide commemoration, but this one never did. The minister of culture would later tell Rwandans that Kizito should not be regarded as a celebrity any longer.

The ruling party is hence determined to control the narrative of the genocide as a black-and-white, Hollywood-like, simplistic version of the events in which Hutus killed Tutsis and the Rwanda Patriotic Army heroically liberated the country and stopped the genocide—completely ignoring grey areas. They hire expensive public relations, marketing experts, and lobbyists to coin and help win this narrative battle. During my stay in Washington, D.C., I met a random tourist who told me he had worked with the Rwandan government to develop a good story to talk about Rwanda's successful recovery from ashes of the genocide to reconciliation and prosperity. This claim has evidence in the economic growth and stability that the country has enjoyed since 1994. Health and education indicators have improved, and the government has demonstrated an ambitious vision to transform the country from an agrarian economy to a skill-based, service-led economy.

There have also been efforts to aid reconciliation. I witnessed some of these efforts when I worked with Never Again Rwanda. Some of the associations the organization supported were made up of genocide survivors and ex-detainees. But the reconciliation that has improved is a horizontal one between individuals, mostly genocide survivors forgiving genocide perpetrators. The reconciliation that is yet to take place, and that still breeds anxiety among Rwandans, is the vertical one between innocent people, mostly self-identified Hutus and the current ruling party, the Rwanda Patriotic Front.

Though there is no evidence that this is what they intend to do, my guess is that they plan to stay in power long enough for all the military leaders who are responsible for these crimes to pass on, and maybe issue an apology when there is no one to prosecute. The truth is that if these grievances are not addressed, they could throw the country back into the abyss of ethnic divisions and violence. With the current efforts to deny reality and prevent innocent young people from voicing their suffering, the RPF has chosen suppression, and we can only hope that people have forgiven them, or feel too powerless to demand justice.

The problem is that this choice legitimizes killing innocent Hutus, and encourages Tutsis to feel that Hutus deserved to suffer. This, in turn leads to dangerous generalizations and discourages the empathy that is needed for genuine reconciliation to take place. In addition, the Rwanda Patriotic Front struggles to be a neutral leader of all Rwandans, since technically the RPF are liberators of Tutsis, and punishers of Hutus. After all, the RPF was founded by Tutsi refugees and is still led mostly by them. They are widely perceived not as neutral leaders, but as Tutsis taking their turn to lead the country after decades of Hutu rule that culminated in the genocide. It follows that there is a presumption on the part of many in power that if they let the Hutus lead, they might lose all access to power. To end this situation will require a much higher moral campus, which is sadly out of the realm of mainstream politics. Politicians are also dealing with their own traumas and biases, and until they heal, they won't be able to truly unify the country—to be *impartial* leaders of *all* Rwandans.

Pressure from foreign judges in France and Spain to prosecute them will only make things worse. What Rwandans need is an honest dialogue and reconciliation among themselves, acknowledgement of all the crimes that were committed, including those committed by those associated with the current ruling class, and an apology from the Rwanda Patriotic Front. Prosecuting RPF top leaders might not make the country more unified, but neither will down-playing war crimes committed against Hutus and some Tutsis. Only radical truth, reconciliation, and forgiveness will unify Rwandans. However long it will take, these three pillars should be the aim.

Igihango: Forging a New Identity, and Thinking as a Nation-State

For this struggle to have meaning, the oppressed must not,
in seeking to regain their humanity
(which is way to create it), become in turn oppressors of the
oppressors, but rather restorers of the humanity of both.

—Paulo Freire

In my thinking about my country's past and its future, I've continued to wrestle with questions political philosophers like Thomas Hobbes and John Locke have debated for centuries, such as, "To what extent should we patiently obey rulers, especially those who are not very good?" and, "To what extent should we start revolutions and depose governments in search of a better world?" All in all, I believe constructive and non-violent means to resolve conflicts are more durable, and therefore these should be the sole means to address grievances of any sort between

227

Rwandans.

The plague of violent nationalist and other identity conflicts around the world is proof that the human species has not escaped the evolutionary paradigm. Studies still show that social organisms are hardwired to make dichotomies about the world. Our brains have evolved to categorize between those organisms that count as "us," and those who count as "them," a means of social organization that has been observed virtually across all social primates. As soon as we are manipulated to think of some people as members of our in-group, we tend to overstate their goodness, and overlook their faults. Equally, when we identify people as out-group members, we exaggerate their vices and downplay their virtues.

I've become convinced that until we evolve beyond seeing our purpose in life as just passing on genes and caring only for the members of our in-group, we will not achieve world peace, unity, and prosperity. Most people are more likely to sacrifice an out-group member, and to save an in-group member, and our brains respond to this binary categorization in milliseconds. The good news is that this dichotomization defect is dynamic. We can re-categorize those who count as "us" and those who count as "them." If the in-grouping criterion is race in the first instance, it turns out that if we learn that someone from a different race supports the same sports team as we do, we can immediately include them in our new in-group and start empathizing with them. Therefore, appealing to and echoing what we have in common is our best bet to guard against future divisiveness.

Today, it behooves the young generation of Rwandans to forge a national identity that puts the Rwandan identity first. But this will not happen unless healing takes place. There are still many young people with unhealed wounds of the genocide and war. Trauma creates distortions, so without healing, truth will not come out. It is every Rwandan's responsibility to acknowledge the suffering of their fellow countrymen, and to understand that the young generation did not commit or support the genocide or the retaliation killings by the RPF.

A simple conversation grounded in the tenets of restorative justice like this could improve trust:

> I know I was young, or unborn, at the time of the genocide and war, but I would like to tell you that I do not support the crimes that were committed against you and your family. You were innocent, and no one should ever experience what you went through. I do not support the genocide committed by Hutus, nor the retaliation killings against innocent civilians by the RPA. All those who committed crimes do not represent me, and I have no sympathy for them. It is unfortunate our country had to go through this, and I hope we can unite and move on.

The other person could respond:

> Thank you for being so open about your feelings. I would like to let you know that I have always wanted to connect with you, and I lacked courage to do so every time I remembered that your family might have supported— either passively or actively—the genocide against the Tutsis or the killings by some RPF soldiers.

A genuine conversation like this could remove doubts and mistrust and lead to authentic reconciliation among young people. A mindset that puts the country's interests over personal grievances would make a difference. Durable reconciliation will require that all forms of discrimination or exclusion (covert or overt) on the basis of "ethnicity" are eliminated. This should go as far as guarding against beauty standards that inadvertently allude to one group being more attractive than the other, and to all other prejudices and stereotypes that helped lead Rwanda to experience genocide and civil war.

One of the lessons we should learn as Rwandans is the commitment to peace, not just within our boundaries, but world-wide. We should refrain from a realist foreign policy that only looks at our interests, sometimes to the detriment of regional, continental, or global stability. Even if Rwanda was abandoned by the global community to self-destruct, Rwandans should be global citizens. Our country has the responsibility to work toward more regional, continental, and global peace, along with fostering stability and cooperation.

Can Rwanda Tell a Story of the Genocide and War That Is Inclusive?

Myths have been essential in nation-building. Narratives of how nations were created unified people around a common cultural and historical heritage. These stories usually included elements of crisis and victory in which members of a nation suffered and triumphed together. Believing in these narratives has had the tremendous ability to forge a common identity, but these narratives have often left out truths about injustices suffered by minorities and the less powerful. This is true in the United States of America, where, for a very long time, Thanksgiving stories mischaracterized the circumstances of the contact between European settler colonialists and Native Americans. Today, that history is being rewritten and many states are celebrating Indigenous People's Day in lieu of Columbus Day.

Likewise, African Americans are increasingly demanding that the country celebrate Juneteenth, the day slavery was last abolished in the state of Texas, and generally African Americans emancipated. America, like many parts of the world, is struggling to rewrite a more inclusive story to unify a country that is becoming more and more diverse, and where minority voices are being heard.

Rwanda will also have to tell a whole story of "ethnic" strife, in which those who sacrificed their lives or stood up against hate, scapegoating, and othering are celebrated as the true heroes, like the Nyanza students who refused to be separated along "ethnic" affiliations and were "martyred" by radical Hutu rebels.

That narrative will also include Tutsis, who, despite suffering at the hands of Hutu radicals, continue to refuse to generalize and blame an entire group of people. These Tutsis also include RPF members and soldiers who, despite witnessing the inhumanity that radical Hutus had unleashed on their families and "ethnic" in-group, resisted retaliating against innocent Hutus.

That narrative will recognize the weakness of those who chose senseless killings, revenge, and scapegoating. It will condemn them, not celebrate them.

It will label them as cowards who betrayed the cause, not heroes who avenged their loved ones. It will say how they succumbed to their primeval instincts and bought into the polarization of the conflict by the radical right, killing even children they assumed were the enemy.

It will condemn those who fell into the trap of the radical right who wanted Hutus to believe in the inhumanity and cruelty of Tutsi.

These radical Hutus knew that by linking all Tutsis to the Tutsi-dominated Rwanda Patriotic Front rebellion, they could convince all Hutus that even civilians were supportive of the rebellion.

But most importantly, Rwanda, like the rest of the world, will need an outline for the story it wants to write. It is this story of the future that will unify Rwanda, not the story of the past. It is the story of unity, reconciliation, and forgiveness. It is the story of a new identity of Rwandanness and humanness. The past controls us, limits our hopes, thoughts, dreams, and imagination, which can limit the horizon of possibilities we can envision. The only reason to revisit the past should be to free ourselves from its chains.

CONCLUSION

We are not enemies, but friends. We must not be enemies.
Though passion may have strained, it must not break our
bonds of affection. The mystic chords of memory... will yet
swell... when again touched, as surely they will be, by the
better angels of our nature.

—Abraham Lincoln

The publication of this book comes five years after my
arrival in the United States. I have told my story and named my
perpetrators. I've had time to heal my wounds and define my
identity for myself. I am neither Tutsi, nor Hutu.

To be honest, I did not fully estimate the cost of my choice
to tell my story and claim my identity: I had to leave everyone
I cared about and everything behind, to become an alien. I
had no idea what it would be like to become a refugee and an
alien resident during a time of heightened nationalism and
xenophobia in the West. I naively thought I would become
invisible in America, since there were no Hutus and Tutsis.

I had no idea I would become Black. I knew I was dark-
skinned, but this was never something I was reminded of in
Rwanda, nor something I had to mention on government
forms. "Black" was not an identity in Rwanda. Everyone was
Black. And even if I tried, I could not be anything other than
Black in the United States. My Blackness is in my DNA and on
my face. In Rwanda I could be vague about my so-called ethnic
identity, but in America it would be ignorant and naïve to say I
wasn't Black. America is a racialized society in which everything

235

is defined in racial terms, from the arts, to politics, and even love (e.g. Black love). I was miserably unprepared to be Black in America.

My life in the United States has been such a paradox. On one hand, most people I've met have been incredibly gracious to me. Many have become like family. On the other hand, I am still considered an alien by the government and treated as a second-class citizen. But at least I am safe here. Although I miss my family and friends in Rwanda, the thought of going back still terrifies me. I pray that one day the political elite will put the sword back in its sheath and truly live up to the slogan of "Never Again." I wish this for the Rwandan people, and also, specifically, for myself, that I might return healed and whole, if only as a visitor, to see that same healing and wholeness manifested across the thousand hills of the land where I was born.

ACKNOWLEDGEMENTS

Writing this memoir has been both therapeutic and gratifying. I am eternally grateful to everyone who somehow contributed to making this project possible.

I am forever indebted to the Connolly family for hosting me in their beautiful home in Sedona while I finalized the manuscript of this book. Your love and hospitality gave me the state of mind I needed to heal and write from a place of fairmindedness.

To Megan St. Marie and Ali de Groot at Modern Memoirs for being empathetic editors who treated my story like a precious newborn baby and not a product to be commercialized.

To my family. To my dad: I am sorry I disobeyed you by running away from my country and going public about the crimes I survived. I would have loved to be "wise" and cautious like you, but my mom's genes of stubbornness won this time. I hope that, at least, I have been as truthful, reconciliatory, and forbearing as you always taught me to be. To my sister Lily for stepping into our mom's shoes so graciously even though you were only two years older than me. To my sister Roseline for always being the kindhearted one. To my brothers Valery, Thierry, and Gentil for copying everything I did, which always reminded me to be a good role model.

Many thanks, as well, to my friends who believed in me and proofread my manuscript or urged me on: Val, Sharath, Kaley, Bill, and Marie.

Finally, to my mother's angels: Fran, Betty, Jim, Joanna,

Auntie Cyndie and Uncle Gary, Mama Nonci, Mama Blandine, Mama Lise, Mama Kathy, and the Landry family. I thank you all for showering me with love and support, and for being my family away from home.